# Welcome to MOONIFESTING

This sacred guide, journal, planner (and everything in between) belongs to the incredible:

Copyright © 2021 Erin Furner

All rights reserved. No part of this book may be reproduced in any form or by an electronic or mechanical means, including information storage and retrieval systems, without permission in writing from the author/publisher (Erin Furner), except by a reviewer who may quote brief passages in a review.

The intent of the author is only to offer information of a general nature to help you on your quest for creating the life you are so deserving of whilst prioritising self-care and self-love. In the event you use any of the information in this book for yourself, which is your constitutional right, the author assumes no responsibility for your actions. The author shall in no event be held liable for any loss or damages, including but not limited to special, incidental, consequential, or other damages.

ISBN: 978-0-9941649-2-6

First Edition: April 2021

10 9 8 7 6 5 4 3 2 1

# Moonifesting:

*Harnessing the power of the Moon and it's phases to cultivate the experience of what it is you truly want - then taking spiritually aligned action so you can allow it to come into form*

Haven't we all looked up at the Moon at least once in our lifetime and marveled at just how beautiful and mysterious it is? Some would say the Moon is just a rock in the sky that controls the tides and while that is true, I believe like so many ancient teachings that there's more to the Moon than meets the eye.

Let's just say she's a powerful force! One that can greatly influence our emotions, behaviour, and consciousness. As the Sun is the yang or masculine energy archetype which represents our outer world (ego or personality), the Moon is the yin or feminine energy archetype which represents our deepest desires, hidden emotions, and shadows. This kind of energy is the beginning of all human-made creations.

Look around you right now. I mean it - *really* do it. What do you see or sense in this moment? Become aware of what's in your hands (including this journal), what you're sitting or standing on, and any other objects and structures that surround you. How do you think they all came to be? Virtually everything that surrounds you was once an idea - an inspiring thought or an intuitive nudge. These ideas were the work of feminine energy before the masculine energy (the one that takes action) could turn it into something tangible. Since the Moon is symbolic of the same feminine energy where ideas and inspiration arise, we can harness it's power to create those big and small changes we've been wanting. We can plant seeds of intention and create new habits, start new projects, and initiate life changes. Not only that but we can propel those changes even further while ensuring we're getting out of our own way. Pretty cool right?!

So this journal will help you do just that; align your life to flow with each of the Moon phases so you learn and grow into the best version of yourself and create the greatest and most fulfilling life possible.

Manifesting such a life can be tricky without a trusted compass guiding the way. Believe me, I know how easy it is to get distracted or dissuaded from walking a certain path especially if it's an unfamiliar one! It's during those times of doubt and fear when I've needed something to keep me focused and on track because if I don't have those things, I lose sight of what I'm doing and why I'm doing it. I've also needed something to help break my protective shell - the one that holds me back because it believes that change is scary and uncertainty should be feared. Maybe you have that same shell too - lots of people do! But if we don't allow ourselves to break open then we learn nothing about ourselves or our potential; life stays the same but that's not what we signed up for when we chose to be human.

So this is why the Moonifesting journal was born - to help you find the clarity in what you want and the courage to get it in the most simplest and easiest way possible. There are 5 important sections in this journal so let's explore them briefly before you dive deeper into this new and exciting adventure of growing into your greatest self.

## 1 The Moon Phases

This is the beginning of co-creating the life you truly desire. In this section you'll find a beautiful graphic of the Northern and Southern Hemisphere Moon Phases, an undated Moon Phase Calendar for you to complete, and a comprehensive spiritual guide on the 8 Moon phases that you'll align your life to.

## 2 The Moon Ritual

As you work with the Moon and it's phases, you'll likely want to create a special kind of Moon ritual. I've included some ways you can do this however they're just suggestive steps. As with all things in this journal, there are no concrete rules, only a basic structure that you may wish to follow.

## ③ Soulful *Practices*

This journal often focuses on self care because it's such a vital ingredient to creating the life you want, so the first part of the Soulful Practices section is the Self Care Agreement. Do not move any further ahead in the journal until you have lovingly completed the agreement (this is very important!). Throughout the journal, there are prompts that will guide you back to the Soulful Practices section. These serve to remind you of the importance of looking out for yourself and creating those high vibes that attract more of what you're looking for. You'll even find oracle card layouts which can be really helpful during times of confusion, procrastination, or if you're seeking general insight into what's really going on in your life.

## ④ The Desires *Road Map*

This is where it gets really exciting! Here you'll be taking a look at your life to see how harmonious and balanced it is. This will help you decide what it is you truly want in life before working with the Moon cycles.

## ⑤ Let the Moonifesting *Begin*

The rest of the journal consists of 6 lunar cycles (closely related to 6 months) where you'll be actively surrendering what you no longer need and opening yourself up to receive all that you desire and deserve. You'll be working with each phase of the Moon (8 phases per cycle) and be guided by regular journal prompts (answering them is optional), soothing meditations, and soul-led affirmations to keep you on track. Before each new lunar cycle begins, you'll find a Lunar Cycle Plan (similar to a monthly plan) to help you see your goals, intentions, habits and moods from a birds-eye view. The first lunar cycle includes an depth description of each of the Moon phases and how they apply to you, while the rest of the journal includes simple journaling prompts and activities without the in-depth descriptions. You could say the first lunar cycle is like riding a bike with training wheels. It just takes a bit of time to get used to before those training wheels come off and you can freely ride into the sunset (or moonlight in this case).

# FAQ's of Moonifesting

**What should I do first?** I recommend you become familiar with the meaning of the Moon phases before jumping into the Moonifesting portion of this journal. Then when you feel comfortable and ready, go ahead and complete the Moon Phase Calendar and the First Desires Road Map activity.

**I'm ready to start Moonifesting but if I do it now it'll be in the middle of the current Moon cycle. What should I do?** Sit tight and wait until the next New Moon begins so you can start fresh whilst the journal guides you through the rest of the cycle.

**What if I miss a phase because of other life commitments?** If you only missed a phase a day or so ago, that's okay. You can still do the activities but just keep in mind that the lunar energy mightn't be as potent especially during the Full Moon. If missing a phase seems to be a regular thing, you might want to reflect on whether you're making yourself a priority. And if you're not, consider why that may be - perhaps your answer is something you could work on during the next lunar cycle.

**Do I need to answer all the questions found in the journal prompts of this book?** No, not at all. The questions in the journal prompts serve as additional offerings to what is already a comprehensive journal. They're written to help you dive deeper into your own understanding about your life and your true nature. Personally, I love the journal prompts as it's helpful to be asked questions that aren't necessarily explored in day-to-day life, but if you're not wanting that kind of experience, then that's totally fine too. You may like to answer them eventually but not necessarily during the particular Moon phase. Remember, this is *your* journal and so it's *your* journey.

**I struggle reading the meditations and doing them at the same time. What can I do?** Me too! That's why I normally record myself reading the meditation first and then I can play it back later on. Recording the meditations are great because you can keep doing them as regularly as you want to. But if that doesn't suit you, ask a family member or friend to read it for you instead.

# MOON PHASES
*Harnessing The Power of The Moon*

It takes about a month for the Moon to orbit Earth (27.3 days to complete a revolution, but 29.5 days to change from New Moon to New Moon). And during that time you'll see the appearance of the Moon change (these are called Moon phases) depending on it's angle and position in relation to the Earth and the Sun. During the day you can even see the different phases of the Moon except for the Full Moon (which is usually only visible at night) and the New Moon (which isn't visible from Earth at all).

There are **eight Moon phases** in total which you'll learn about in this section. Each phase has a spiritual meaning that we can align our lives too. Becoming knowledgeable about these Moon phases is the first step along the path of co-creating the life you truly desire. I say *co-creating* because you'll be partnering up with your spiritual counterpart whether it be the Universe, God, Creator, Source, All That Is - whatever name you resonate with. This spiritual counterpart will gladly open doors and show you pathways to undertake along the way if you're willing to accept a helping hand.

By understanding the phases of a Moon cycle (also known as a Lunar cycle), you can use this journal to it's fullest and reflect on your own life, explore what is stirring within you, and what is holding you back. And as these are cycles, it means they continue to repeat while you continue to learn, grow and evolve.

In the first part of The Moon Phase section, you'll see how the **Moon phases of the Southern and Northern hemisphere** appear in the sky depending on your geographic location. Despite the change in appearance, it doesn't change the spiritual meaning of each phase - it's purely to align what you see in the sky to what you complete in your **Moon Phase Calendar**. The Moon Phase Calendar will help you know when to take part in a particular activity within the journal. Since this is an undated journal, it means you can start anytime of the year. Who says it's all about New Years resolutions when you can make a new resolution any day! You can find the dates for each of the Moon phases on many websites including my own. Then it's just a matter of recording the dates in your Moon Phase Calendar and you're all set!

When the particular Moon phase appears in your geographic location, you can jump to the same Moon phase within this book to take part in the guidance offered. But just remember that it's best to start when it's the New Moon as that signifies the beginning of the Moonifesting cycle and so it will be easier to follow and apply the guidance and wisdom found within these pages.

So, are you ready to work with the natural energetic forces and rhythmicity of the Moon to manifest your ideal life? Thought so! Let's begin.

# MOON PHASES
## of the *Southern Hemisphere*

**1. NEW MOON**
New beginnings
Unlimited Possibilities
Seeds of intention

**2. WAXING CRESCENT**
Focus
Intention
Motivation
Curiosity

**3. FIRST QUARTER**
Flexibility
Challenges
Decisions
Action

**4. WAXING GIBBOUS**
Edit + refine
Refocus
Open to change
Patience

**5. FULL MOON**
Release setbacks
Celebrate
Momentum
Self-love

**6. WANING GIBBOUS**
Gratitude
Enthusiasm
Give back
Love fully

**7. THIRD QUARTER**
Release
Let go
Forgiveness
Cleanse

**8. WANING CRESCENT**
Surrender
Reflection
Trust
Rest + restore

Inspiration
Transformation
Creative Action
Manifestation

# MOON PHASES
## of the Northern Hemisphere

**1. NEW MOON**
New beginnings
Unlimited Possibilities
Seeds of intention

**2. WAXING CRESCENT**
Focus
Intention
Motivation
Curiosity

**8. WANING CRESCENT**
Surrender
Reflection
Trust
Rest + restore

Inspiration | Transformation

**3. FIRST QUARTER**
Flexibility
Challenges
Decisions
Action

**7. THIRD QUARTER**
Release
Let go
Forgiveness
Cleanse

Creative Action | Manifestation

**4. WAXING GIBBOUS**
Edit + refine
Refocus
Open to change
Patience

**6. WANING GIBBOUS**
Gratitude
Enthusiasm
Give back
Love fully

**5. FULL MOON**
Release setbacks
Celebrate
Momentum
Self-love

MOONIFESTING

# MOON Phase

**January**

○ ○ ○ ○ ○ ○ ○ ○ ○

Date
___

**February**

○ ○ ○ ○ ○ ○ ○ ○ ○

Date
___

**March**

○ ○ ○ ○ ○ ○ ○ ○ ○

Date
___

**April**

○ ○ ○ ○ ○ ○ ○ ○ ○

Date
___

**May**

○ ○ ○ ○ ○ ○ ○ ○ ○

Date
___

**June**

○ ○ ○ ○ ○ ○ ○ ○ ○

Date
___

**Notes**

---

**Moon Phase Appearance Key for the Sourthern Hemisphere**

Record the date and colour in the blank circles to reflect each Moon phase

○ New Moon     Waxing Crescent     First Quarter     Waxing Gibbous     Full Moon     Waning Gibbous     Last Quarter     Waning Crescent

# CALENDAR

**July** ◯ ◯ ◯ ◯ ◯ ◯ ◯ ◯ ◯
Date _____

**August** ◯ ◯ ◯ ◯ ◯ ◯ ◯ ◯ ◯
Date _____

**September** ◯ ◯ ◯ ◯ ◯ ◯ ◯ ◯ ◯
Date _____

**October** ◯ ◯ ◯ ◯ ◯ ◯ ◯ ◯ ◯
Date _____

**November** ◯ ◯ ◯ ◯ ◯ ◯ ◯ ◯ ◯
Date _____

**December** ◯ ◯ ◯ ◯ ◯ ◯ ◯ ◯ ◯
Date _____

**Notes**

---

**Moon Phase Appearance Key for the Northern Hemisphere**

Record the date and colour in the blank circles to reflect each Moon phase

New Moon | Waxing Crescent | First Quarter | Waxing Gibbous | Full Moon | Waning Gibbous | Last Quarter | Waning Crescent

MOONIFESTING

# NEW MOON
## Plant New Seeds of Intentions

The New Moon brings about new beginnings. Since the energy around this phase is focused on starting fresh, it's no wonder why it's commonly referred to as the beginning of the Lunar Month (Synodic month). One lunar month averages 29 and a half days which is the time it takes for the Moon to pass through each of her phases from New Moon, to Full Moon, and back to New Moon.

In the darkness of the New Moon, you'll be gathering your thoughts, shaking off what may have happened in previous months, and consciously creating new heartfelt desires for the coming month, season, or year. During this fertile period of preparation and planning, you'll be creating the necessary space to infuse potential as you breathe life into the seeds of ideas, inspiration and dreams.

As you work with the energy of the New Moon, try not to get caught up on *how* your goals will manifest into reality (that's the job of the Universe) but instead, focus on planting the seeds of intention whilst maintaining trust that the Universe will provide you with the necessary water, sunlight and nutrients to bring life to those seeds (aka your dreams). As the Moon cycles through her phases, you'll know in time when it's necessary to take action.

*Everything that belongs in my life is making it's way towards me right now*

# WAXING CRESCENT
*Fine Tune Your Intentions and Goals*

The Waxing Crescent signifies motivation and focus as you fine tune your intentions, lay out a plan, and start to take spiritually inspired action. As the Moon's illumination grows during this time, the energy around your intentions, goals and envisioning's start to build.

This is a period where you'll be allowing your dreams and curiosity to be your guide in bringing your desires into form. You might find fears and doubts show up unexpectedly which may tempt you to reconsider whether what you're striving for is achievable. But instead of giving in to such limiting beliefs, take pleasure in the feeling of experiencing what the manifestation of your desires will feel like from the inside out.

Invite magic into your life, believe in possibilities, and be open to the gifts and synchronistic opportunities that the Universe is constantly sending you. When opportunities show up or you have an idea that comes to mind, then use this time to act upon it. The energy around the Waxing Crescent is one of movement. So as you become proactive in laying the groundwork for your desires to flourish, keep in mind what you could be doing now to move you closer to fulfilling your desires and why you're wanting what you're working for because it's the *why* that builds the momentum.

*I am an energetic match to everything I want*

# FIRST QUARTER
## Make Decisions and Take Action

The First Quarter phase symbolises decision making. Your seed of intention is now starting to take root and grow into a plant-like structure. This of course is a period of strength, determination, and commitment to action.

During this phase you'll be spending your time creating a to-do list and actively checking it off as you go. Because this phase typically stirs up frustration and lack of motivation, it's important to stay laser focused on your goals and remind yourself of *why* you're doing this. As obstacles and challenges occur which can delay or obscure your plans, be prepared to make decisions on the spot instead of getting caught up on what's not going well. Give yourself the permission and space to remain flexible as you work with the energies of the Moon and the Universe.

Understandably it can be tempting to work on multiple goals to try to achieve them sooner however this can create confusion, overwhelm, and unnecessary stress, so avoid taking on too much as you fine tune the steps needed to turn your dreams into reality.

Not only can having multiple goals create overwhelm but so can assigning multiple tasks to fulfill just one goal. This is why the First Quarter section of this journal focuses on writing down the *first 3 tasks* needed to get you closer to your goal rather than trying to write down every single task (because that would be stressful!). The beauty of this is that when you have completed those 3 tasks, you can go ahead and add another 3, and so on. Goodbye overwhelm! And remember; if there's ever a time you feel an overload of negativity, use your creative passions to bust right through it.

*I am a do-er. I take spiritually inspired action and get things done easily and naturally*

# WAXING GIBBOUS
*Refine and Make Changes if Needed*

The Waxing Gibbous phase symbolises refinement of your goals. As a greater percentage of the Moon is illuminated by the Sun, this is the time to make edits, refocus and decide if there's anything in your plan that needs to be changed to accomplish your goals. Take what you have learnt so far during this cycle, gather all the information, and then decide on where your focus should lie.

As you refine and make the necessary changes, it's important to continue to check in with your inner knowing and trust your own innate wisdom (if it feels right, it likely is). You can also request a sign or signal from the Universe to help you decide what the best course of action is.

If you realise your plans aren't coming together and no amount of time or energy spent on those plans will help you move forward, then that's completely okay! Try to avoid being critical on yourself or critical toward the process; simply trust that even when things change, it's just an opportunity for self growth, expansion, and something better to come your way.

Place trust in the Universe and have patience as the finer details of your goals continue to illuminate.

*I surrender the outcome of my goals to the Universe whilst maintaining peace within*

# FULL MOON
## Release Setbacks and Seal Your Intentions

The Full Moon is the most powerful lunar phase and symbolises the realisation and fulfillment of your desires. When the illumination of the Moon shines light on your intentions and goals, the full extent of your plans may be revealed. This makes it easier to see if your goals need to be further tweaked and if they do, now is the perfect time to do it.

During this phase it's quite common for emotional energies and tension to be high. So even though you're continuing to evaluate your goals and plans, it's important to clear your mind and allow the energies to flow through you. When heightened emotions are experienced, take it easy on yourself. Avoid stressing yourself out and doing anything that causes you more tension. Ultimately, you'll be replacing some of the tasks on your to-do list with self-love practices.

You may find old wounds from your past, negatives thoughts, and bad habits are easier to spot at this time (these are called your Shadows - you'll be doing what's called Shadow Work during this Moon phase which will be explained further in this journal) so be kind and gentle to yourself as you bring healing to those parts of self. This is an important step because as you bring resolution to your life, you create space for expansion, abundance, joy and happiness.

*I release all that no longer serves my highest good and purpose in life. Now is the time. I am unstoppable.*

# WANING GIBBOUS
## Appreciate All That is

The Waning Gibbous phase symbolises gratitude, sharing, and enthusiasm toward your desires. As the Moon starts to decrease in illumination, it's the perfect time to reap the benefits of the work you've been doing and bring the manifestation of your desires to closure. This is also a great time to declutter your life in a physical, emotional, and spiritual sense.

Since the energy around Waning Gibbous is one of gratitude, it's a wonderful time to share the love that's rising within you and your appreciation for this journey with others. Nothing expands your energy more than sharing your good vibes with the people in your life or reconnecting with those you may have neglected or been a bit rude to.

Being grateful for your life can also mean it's time to look inward to explore what may be weighing you down and what the gift is behind those things. Since every experience (good or bad) has an opportunity for spiritual growth, this is the perfect time to find closure in old patterns and past memories that are no longer serving your highest potential. It's also a time to reflect on whether your goals are for the good of others as well as for yourself.

*I am constantly reminded of just how much there is to be grateful for*

# THIRD QUARTER
## *Release and Forgive*

The Third Quarter phase is one of release, letting go, and forgiveness. As the Moon's illumination continues to decrease, you'll be ready to let go of low vibe energy. Through the lunar cycle you may have been hurt, disappointed, broken or angered in different ways, so now is the time to let go of any pent up emotions that cause suffering. This will help you create space for creativity and growth during the next stage of creating new intentions and goals.

Think of this phase as a cleansing one where you'll be decluttering your life; your environment, relationships, money, emotional, spiritual, and physical health. Look at anything in your life that's not serving your highest potential and let it go. Sometimes this may require you to forgive a certain person or situation in order to be free from it, so before attempting to let it go, make sure there isn't any unfinished business. Physical activity or attending a class that focuses on shifting stagnant and pent up emotions may be really useful during this time.

Now the seeds have grown and the benefits have been reaped, it's time to stop, contemplate, soul-search, reflect, and re-evaluate for your future. Surrender to the Universe and take some time to align to the energy of calm.

*When I let go of all that no longer serves me, I create space for something better*

# WANING CRESCENT
## *Reflect and Surrender*

The Waning Crescent relates to a period of surrender. As the Moon's illumination diminishes, you'll be using this time to become a non-judgmental observer of all aspects of your life to ensure there aren't any areas that feel stifled, strained, or in a state of struggle. What you're aiming for is balance and this is something that will continue to flow through to the next lunar cycle.

This is also a time to rest and not become tempted to start planning your future. You've gone through the entire lunar cycle and things may or may not have gone as well as planned. Use this time to take extra care of yourself and try not to control the world around you as this will only interrupt your ability to find peace and calm.

As you bring closure to this lunar cycle, honour and love your strengths, realisations, accomplishments, and even your shadows (the parts of self that you mightn't want to admit to having) so that you can choose to not let those old stories and patterns stop you from radiating your soul's light onto others.

This is your chance to connect to the greater potential of your soul where the courage lies in following your deepest desires.

*I surrender control over what I feel should be and entrust the Universe for the path it puts in front of me*

# THE MOON RITUAL
## How to Do a Moon Ritual

A ritual is simply an activity you do with intention and care. It's when you're fully focused and mindful of the activity without allowing any distractions to pull you away from what's important. When you think about it, using this journal is a type of ritual. But if sitting in your favourite chair as you devour this journal during each of the Moon phases doesn't quite feel sacred enough, then you may like to create a more purposeful space and follow it by saying a prayer before diving into the specific lunar phase activities within these pages.

Included here is a suggested Moon ritual that you can easily do during each Moon phase (but it's not essential). There's also a more specific Moon ritual for the Full Moon which you might like to do. Let's begin!

**You will need:**
Pen to write with
Candle and matches*
Crystal or rock (refer to Crystals to Work With page for recommendations)
Incense or white sage to burn*
One bowl with salt water (add salt to water)
One empty fire-proof bowl* (for the Full Moon phase)
Hand towel

**Optional items:**
Oracle cards or other divination tool
Flowers
Cup of tea or other comforting beverage to place you in a relaxed state
Background relaxation music playing

*Fire safety notice: Ensure you're fully versed in fire safety and have fire safety equipment close by before starting the ritual.

# THE MOON RITUAL
## Creating & Cleansing your Sacred Space

### CREATE YOUR SACRED SPACE

This is simply a personal space indoors or outdoors that you wish to dedicate to the practice of the Moon ritual. In can be, for example, an altar, your kitchen table, an area of grass in your backyard, a warm bath, or your bedside table. Just choose a space that provides you with some privacy and comfort as you do this work. When you have chosen the space, make it beautiful! Keep candles, flowers, incense, crystals, and other symbolic items that create a deep feeling of spiritual connection and inspiration.

### CLEAR YOUR SACRED SPACE

Every item, no matter how big or small, stores psychic energy (including you). If the psychic energy contains a type of negative vibration, then it will likely interfere with the Moonifesting practice. So before taking part in the ritual, it's important to clear yourself and your sacred space by, for example, burning white sage (smoke cleansing), clapping, or ringing a bell. Whatever method you choose, ensure you make a small invocation *before* you clear the space such as...

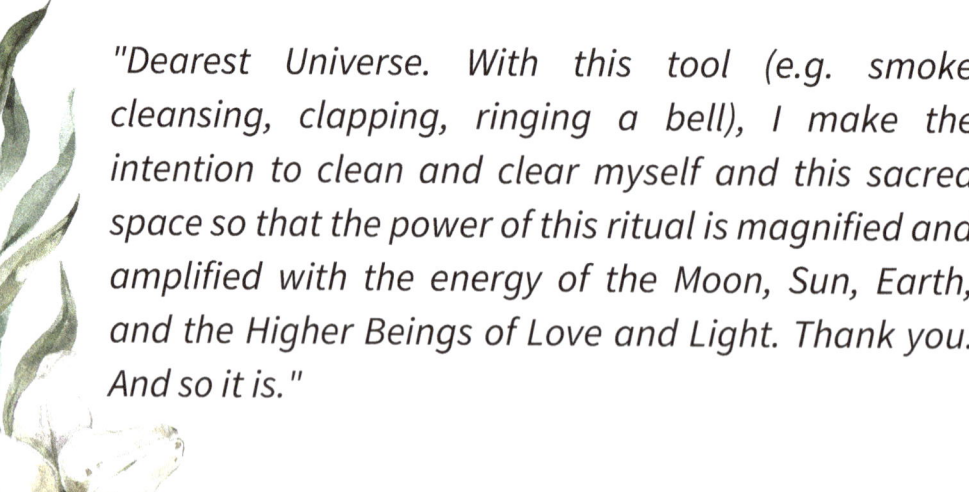

*"Dearest Universe. With this tool (e.g. smoke cleansing, clapping, ringing a bell), I make the intention to clean and clear myself and this sacred space so that the power of this ritual is magnified and amplified with the energy of the Moon, Sun, Earth, and the Higher Beings of Love and Light. Thank you. And so it is."*

# THE MOON RITUAL
*Opening your Sacred Space*

It's time to open your sacred space and begin the Moon ritual. Being that the Moon works in harmony with Mother Earth and the Sun, it's only fitting that you honour the love, support and nourishment received by these entities. By honouring these entities, you also honour yourself since you're an extension of these things (remember that nothing is separate). The way to show your appreciation and respect is to connect to the four elements of Earth.

## HOW TO CONNECT TO THE FOUR ELEMENTS

- **Earth:** Hold your chosen crystal or rock to connect to the vibration of the Earth for a few minutes and then place it near you
- **Fire:** Light your candle/s and witness it's flame
- **Air:** Light your incense or white sage and notice how the smoke moves in the air
- **Water:** Fill a small bowl with water and add some sea salt to represent the Earth's oceans. If you're practicing the ritual in a warm bath, you may like to add some Epsom salt or Himalayan salt to the bath water

Breathe deeply as you sit in or near your sacred space with the intention of bringing awareness to the current lunar phase and energy surrounding it. During this time you may also like to call upon your Spiritual Support team for protection and guidance as you explore your deepest desires, release the blocks, and open yourself up to the free flow of abundant energy.

# THE MOON RITUAL
## Invocation to the Moon

Now that you're grounded and connected to the four elements, it's time to open your sacred space and connect to the Universe. You can do this by making an invocation. An invocation is a beautiful way to bring yourself into the present moment and set an intention to connect with the infinite energy of consciousness (the Universe). By doing this simple practice, you're opening up the pathway of surrendering and receiving.

Below is an example of what you might like to say as you intentionally go about each of the lunar activities. If you feel called, you may like to place your hands on your heart centre or in prayer position as you say the words; feeling each word echo deeply into your being as you speak or think them. You may even like to create your own invocation.

### MOON INVOCATION

*"Dearest Universe; Mother Earth, the Moon, Spiritual Beings of Love and Light. I ask for guidance, clarity, direction, and courage to the know the truth - that I have the power to live in the way my heart deeply desires because I am eternally connected to all things. Let this eternal connection help me shine light on the obstacles and blocks, release and surrender what no longer serves my highest good, strengthen my ability to dream, help me to take inspired action, and encourage me to reconnect to the wholeness of who I am. I am honoured to spend this time receiving your radiance and guiding force as I know it leads me to tap into my own divine essence whilst reminding me of my power, grace, and the innate ability to receive simply because I exist. Thank you. And so it is."*

Now you can follow and complete the specific Moon Phase activities within this journal depending on which phase of the lunar cycle you're working with.

# THE MOON RITUAL
## Closing your Sacred Space

After you have taken part in the particular lunar phase activity within this journal, you will then close your sacred space. Doing something that symbolically represents the end/closing of your ritual is helpful for your unconscious mind to understand that it's over. This is especially important if you had brought awareness to some difficult things in your life particularly during the Full Moon phase where you'll be exploring your shadow self. Closing the ritual is very simple. In fact, it's entirely up to you as to how you want to do it. Here are just a few suggestions but as always, use your own intuition to help you decide on what's best for you.

### Mantra or prayer

You may like to recite your favourite mantra or say a prayer as you sense the energy of the ritual gently closing. You can thank the Moon for it's feminine illumination, Mother Earth for her nourishment and love, the Sun for the masculine life it gives you, and the Universe for making all of this possible.

### Play music

Play some music that helps you stay in a relaxed and peaceful state. You may even want to play a singing bowl or some other form of instrument.

### Express gratitude

You may also like to speak a few words about what you're most grateful for in the moment whether it be for the ritual, releasing the shadows, embracing the new, or anything else that inspires you. Having gratitude and letting it speak through you is a beautiful way of sealing the ritual with high love-filled vibes.

# THE MOON RITUAL
*Full Moon - Shadow Work*

Beneath our social exterior lies hidden parts of ourselves that have been wounded, suppressed, isolated or are impulsive. Since these parts of ourselves can be painful to connect to, it's normal that most of us would prefer to ignore them and hope they won't interfere with our lives. Unfortunately ignoring them doesn't serve any purpose other than making our lives far harder and less enjoyable.

Although it can be hard to admit your shadows and even harder to see, feel and accept them, it's a necessary step to transformation; reclaiming and embodying your true nature (the one that can manifest with ease!). It's good to keep in mind that your shadow self actually holds beautiful gifts for you when you take the time to look.

So how do shadows appear in your life? Anytime there's self sabotage, self absorption or self-loathing; that's a shadow. Anytime there's greed, addictions, hypocrisy, narcissism, intense anxiety, laziness, insecurity, co-dependency, resistance to change, manipulation or aggression; that's a shadow. Of course these are just examples and there are a many more. Ultimately if the shadow self remains hidden, it can lead to feelings of resentment, oppression, anger, guilt, shame, disgust and a general unhappiness without really knowing why.

But help is at hand! Using the energy of the Full Moon, you can bring uncritical and compassionate light to your shadow self, honour it for what it is, and have gratitude for how it has served you in a positive way.

**NOTE:** *If you decide shadow work isn't for you because it's too painful and you're not feeling in a good place right now, then perhaps ask the Universe for help on self-love instead. Although shadow work is a form of self-love, it can be quite polarising so it's important you feel emotionally stable to do this.*

# QUICK MOON RITUAL GUIDE

Step-by-Step

Step 1. Create and open your sacred space as described in this book

Step 2. Clear and ground yourself. Envision white light showering you and washing away any negativity. Imagine the white light then filling your entire body with pure energy

Step 3. Take a few deep breaths and read the Moon Invocation out loud or to yourself with intention and feeling

Step 4. Following the specific Moon phase journal portion of this book

Step 5. **FOR THE FULL MOON:** When you have finished the Shadow Work section, sign and date it and then declare out loud, 'I lovingly accept and release these shadows'

Step 6. **FOR THE FULL MOON:** Remove the Shadow Work page from your journal and light the corner of the page with the candle, drop it into the empty bowl, and let it burn. Watch the flames cleanse and clear all that no longer serves you. If you do not wish to burn the page, you can rip it up into tiny pieces instead and then throw away the pieces into your recycling bin

Step 7. Now place your hands in the bowl of salt water to cleanse your aura; cleansing the old and opening up to the new. Remove your hands from the water and dry them with your hand towel while breathing deeply

Step 8. Sit in silence for a while or journal if you feel called (there's a Notes section at the end of this book to write in)

Step 9. Close the ritual as described in this book

# SELF CARE AGREEMENT

Before you begin to transform your life and reach those big dreams and goals, it's important to look out for #1 (you). Self care is your health care. Without it you'll likely experience disease and unrest which is the complete opposite to living a joyful life! So what can you do? Create a self care agreement! This agreement will become the very thing you can turn to to help manage any stress, tension or anxiety felt throughout the day.

- Reduce screen time before bedtime
- Engage in a non-work hobby
- Make an ultra healthy smoothie
- Do some yoga
- Hug a tree
- Sing out loud
- Drink at least 8 glasses of water
- Go outside barefoot
- Move the body and get active
- Take a nap
- Chat with a friend
- Meditate
- Cry it out
- Listen to your favourite music
- Colour or do art
- Get some fresh air
- Read a few pages of your favourite book
- Sit quietly for 10 minutes
- Dress up for no reason
- Get crafty and make something
- Drink a soothing herbal tea
- Start your day with water
- Take some deep breaths

DO WHAT MAKES YOU FEEL *Good*

MOONIFESTING

# SELF CARE AGREEMENT
*Looking After Myself*

Now it's your turn. Write or draw the Mind, Body, Spirit self care activities you plan to do anytime you need an extra high-vibe energy boost particularly during the stressful and overwhelming moments.

I, _____ hereby declare that I will do these activities anytime I feel stressed or am in need of an extra boost of high-vibes.

Signed: _____ Date: _____

# DECLUTTER
## *A Reminder to Release The Old*

When you have an excess amount of 'stuff' (clutter) in your life, it can bog you down, distract you from the important things, and create unnecessary stress. As your ideas and visions remain wishful thinking, it can make it hard to go after your big goals and dreams let alone know what you truly want in life. Decluttering - cleaning up your physical, mental and emotional state - can free you from those stuck places and help you take inspired action. It helps to harness the free flow of creative energy which, as you'll come to know, is vitally important for your Moonifestation routine.

## HOW DOES IT WORK?

Throughout this journal you'll find Decluttering prompts. These serve to remind you to come back here and choose one or more of the decluttering suggestions. Of course if you have your own in mind, choose them instead! The best way to declutter your life is to take it one step at a time because when you combine the smaller steps you'll find they'll lead to those big improvements you're after.

*When you step into the vibration of overwhelm and agitation from all the 'stuff' in your life, you immediately step out of the vibration of openly receiving and experiencing peace.*

## DECLUTTER YOUR ENVIRONMENT

Here's a great weekly practice you can do to get the 'declutter ball' rolling. Make 6 signs: Keep, Donate, Sell, Trash, Recycle, and Can't Decide. Next, choose a part of the house or even a drawer or cupboard you would like to declutter (just start somewhere!) and place the signs near your chosen space or on empty boxes. Set your timer for one hour and start sorting. Pick up every item one at a time, and ask yourself: Do I use this? Have I used it in the past year? Will I use it again in the next three months? Do I truly love it? Does it have meaning for me? If the answer is No, place the item near the appropriate sign on in one of the boxes, and then let it go.

# DECLUTTER
## Ways to Release the Old

- Be honest about how you feel in each and every single one of your relationships. Consider if the relationship is worth the effort

- Write down all your commitments. Look at each one and decide whether it really brings you joy and value, and if it's worth the amount of time that you invest in it (*don't be afraid to say No to a commitment*)

- Clean out your wallet

- Create a minimalist sanctuary or a space to wind down without the clutter

- Set a limit for using social media and checking emails

- Replace expectations on yourself and others with acceptance and gratitude of what is

- Spend 10 minutes looking through your social media accounts and unfollow anyone who you're no longer aligned with

- Meditate and stay in the moment

- Do an electronic detox e.g. Unsubscribe from email accounts that you never open. For those documents and emails you need to keep, create folders that are categorised just as you would for a paper file

- Remove out of date food and declutter the pantry and refrigerator so good, healthy, and nutritious food is readily accessible and doesn't go bad

- Remove unwanted exercise gizmo's, diet books and other health-related items

- Create a trash journal and write down all your negative thoughts (*but don't re-read them*)

- Think back to your past at a time that was most painful. Then ask yourself, 'What has this experience taught me and how can I improve myself from the lessons learned through this experience?'

- Keep a permanent Donation box. As soon as your box is full, donate the contents to your local charity

- Create a budget and start by keeping a record of all your earnings and outgoings for at least a month. Then you can spot ways to reduce your spending, like bundling your phone and internet, or shopping in bulk

Date:

# GIVE BACK
## *During Waning Gibbous and beyond*

This is the perfect time to share your positive vibes with others. Tick one or more activities you're going to do to spread your high vibes and then go ahead and do them!

- [ ] Give someone a bouquet of flowers
- [ ] Recycle
- [ ] Pick up any rubbish and dispose it properly
- [ ] Write a friendly note and put it in the letterbox of someone you don't know
- [ ] Text or call a friend who you haven't spoken to in a while
- [ ] Be a good listener
- [ ] Ask someone about their day
- [ ] Smile to at least 5 people who you don't know
- [ ] Write a love note to yourself
- [ ] Offer food to someone who really needs it
- [ ] Give items of clothing and other things you no longer want to charity
- [ ] Surprise a friend or family member
- [ ] Buy coffee for the person behind you in the take away line
- [ ] Volunteer your time towards something you're passionate about
- [ ] Other...

# ORACLE CARD SPREAD
*For Spiritual Insight*

The imagery, symbolism and stories that oracle cards reveal can provide such powerful insights into what's *really* going on in your life because it's your inner wisdom (intuition) that brings meaning to each of the cards. And from this place of inner knowing and power, you can discover how to make positive changes to your life so you can manifest your goals and desires.

I've included some really useful oracle card spreads that you can follow as you move through this journal. Anytime you feel stuck and overwhelmed with making a decision, you might like to do the Decision Making spread below. During the New Moon and Full Moon, you might like to do an oracle card spread. A blank journal page has been included for both these Moon phases so you can record the results of your oracle card spread.

If you're not interested in oracle cards, that's completely okay! It won't change the way you'll be navigating through this journal. These oracle card spreads are simply an addition to your journey.

## 3-CARD SPREAD FOR DECISION MAKING

| 1 | 2 | 3 |
|---|---|---|
| Strengths | Weaknesses | Advice |
| Issue | Reason | Action |
| What do I need the most? | What's blocking me? | How do I remove the block? |
| Opportunity | Challenges | Outcome |
| Embrace | Accept | Let go |
| The solution | The alternative solution | How to choose |

# ORACLE CARD SPREAD
## New Moon and Full Moon

**NEW MOON**

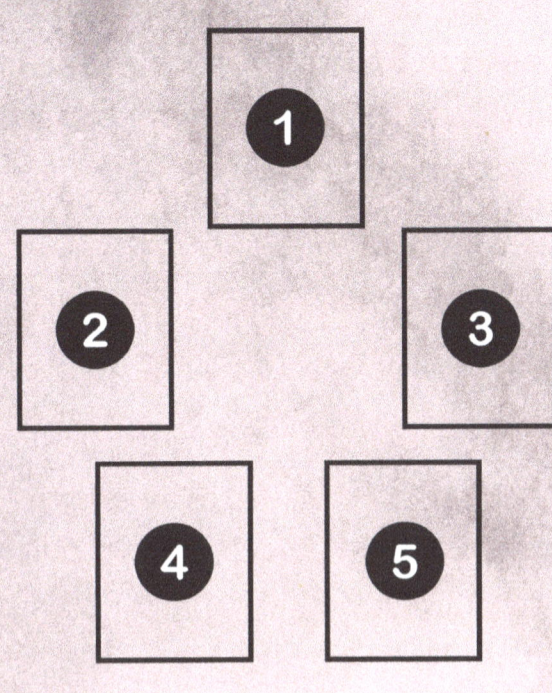

1. Where am I right now in my life?
2. What do I wish to bring into my life?
3. What might be blocking me from growing (what do I need to resolve)?
4. What resources are available to me to manifest my dreams?
5. What positive energy will emerge during this phase and throughout this lunar cycle?

**FULL MOON**

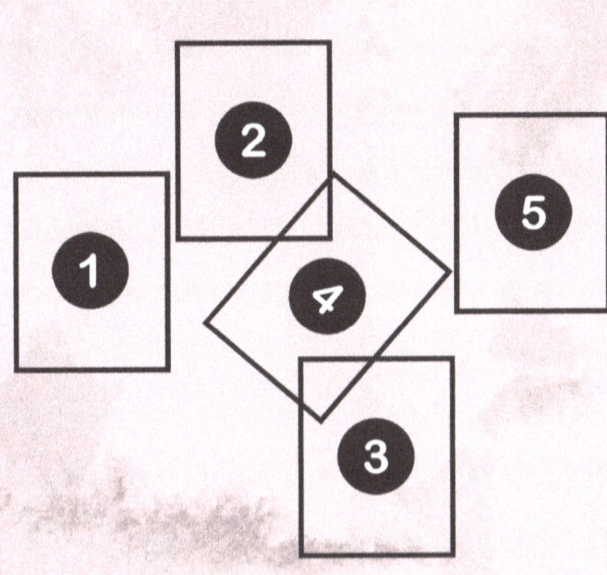

1. Where am I right now during this phase?
2. How may I be in my own way?
3. What other obstacles might I be facing?
4. How can I easily break through these obstacles?
5. What might be waiting for me on the other side of this phase?

# WORKING WITH CRYSTALS
## During Moonifesting

As you step onto this journey of conscious manifestation, you'll soon realise that everything needs a structure to manifest, especially your thoughts and intentions. This is why crystals are such powerful tools to work with when you're Moonifesting. With their crystalline structure, they can absorb, hold and radiate energy that might be hard to obtain elsewhere. And since everything resonates at different frequencies, crystals can bridge those frequencies - bringing your consciousness into harmony with whatever you truly desire in life.

### 1. Choose your Crystal

Over the page I've included some crystals that are known to benefit certain desires as well as common crystals that can be used during each Moon phase. Be mindful that these are suggestions only. There are so many crystals to choose from and ultimately it's up to your intuition to choose the crystal that's vibrating at the frequency you're looking for. Working with crystals is optional but certainly a powerful addition to your Moonifesting repertoire.

### 2. Cleanse your Crystal (aka a crystal reset)

Simply place your crystal where it will be fully exposed to the energising rays of the Full Moon, smudge some white sage over your crystal, or play a tuning fork, Tibetan or crystal singing bowl loudly (it doesn't matter the note played). Do this the first time you've ever used the crystal and then anytime you feel the crystal needs it. Note: if your crystal has absorbed high amplitude such as high emotions; yelling, breaking things, and manic behavior, then it'll need a reset.

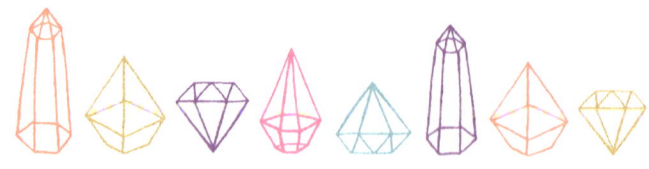

# ③ Work with your *Crystal*

Now that you have decided on which crystal (or crystals) to work with, you can start embracing it's power. Firstly set your intentions of why you're working with this particular crystal. To do this, sit quietly and breathe deeply whilst holding the crystal in your hands. Next, state what you want to manifest. Then each day, hold the crystal while mediating, place it under your pillow at night, pop it on your bedside table, or position it in a sacred space to look at and connect to when you're most relaxed. The options are endless so tune into what works with you and your crystal.

## Moon Phase Crystals

**New Moon**
Labradorite

**Waxing Crescent**
Rose Quartz

**First Quarter**
Carnelian

**Waxing Gibbous**
Smokey Quartz

**Full Moon**
Moonstone

**Waning Gibbous**
Green Adventurine

**Third Quarter**
Aquamarine

**Waning Crescent**
Bloodstone

## Top 10 Must-have Crystals

**Clear Quartz**
Clarity and energy amplification

**Rose Quartz**
Love and compassion

**Fluorite**
Focus and decision making

**Green Jade**
Healing and good fortune

**Amethyst**
Energy protection and peace

**Black Tourmaline**
Transmuting negative energy

**Smokey Quartz**
Detox and release of old wounds

**Blue Calcite**
Calm and spiritual connection

**Natural Hematite**
Grounding and stability

**Natural Citrine**
Creativity and positivity

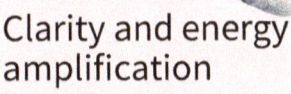

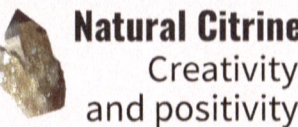

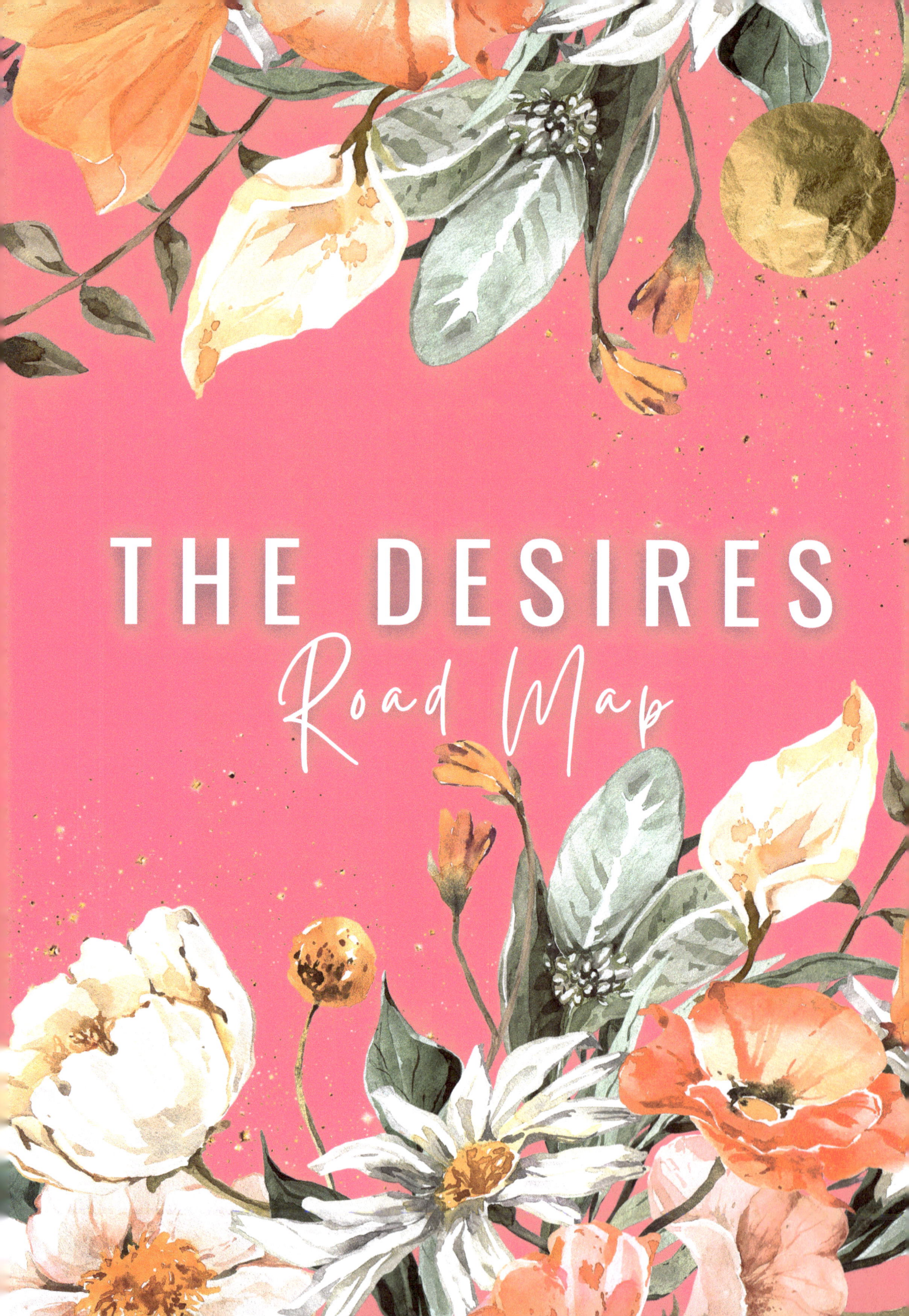

# THE DESIRES ROAD MAP
*The Journey Begins*

To help you transform your life and fulfill your desires, it's necessary to take a look at how harmonious and balanced your life is right now. Because if there are any areas of stagnation and unfulfillment, then you'll likely feel limited to abundance and joy (*we want to avoid that!*).

To gain a clear view of how harmonious and balanced your life is, you'll be using the **Life Balance Wheel**. During this simple exercise, you'll be categorising the deeply important aspects of your life and then scaling them on the wheel to gain an overview of where energy is abundant (*where you may feel joy, happiness, or fulfillment*) and where energy is lacking (*where you may feel unfulfilled, stagnant, or depressed*). You'll then be journaling your insights which will be used to determine what it is you truly want. This creates the ultimate **Desires Road Map**. You'll be creating three Desires Road Maps during the first, third, and fifth lunar cycle because your life will likely change and so the degree of balance may change as well. The journal includes a reminder to do each Desires Road Map (at the beginning of every second New Moon) so you needn't worry about *when* that will be. Just relax and allow this journal (and the Moon + Universe) to show you the way.

Here are some suggested **Life Balance Wheel categories** you may like to use (*or you can use your own*):

| | | |
|---|---|---|
| Home | Social / Friends | Hobbies |
| Relationships | Career / Study | Fun / Recreation |
| Health | Wealth / Finance | Confidence |
| Love | Spiritual / Self-Time | Creativity |
| Family | Contribution | Self Love |

*A gentle reminder...*
*Before you do this exercise, just remember that the NOW is perfect in each and every moment. This means that this exercise is not about seeing how bad you or your life is, but instead which areas could do with a healthy dose of self-devotion, love, reflection and growth.*

MOONIFESTING

Date:

# THE FIRST
# DESIRES ROAD MAP

## MY LIFE BALANCE WHEEL

**You represent the centre of the wheel** and each segment represents each category of your life here on Earth – *as a spiritual being having a physical experience.* Add your categories to each segment and using a scale of 0 - 10 (0 = unfulfilled, 10 = completely fulfilled) colour in how fulfilled, happy and satisfied you are.

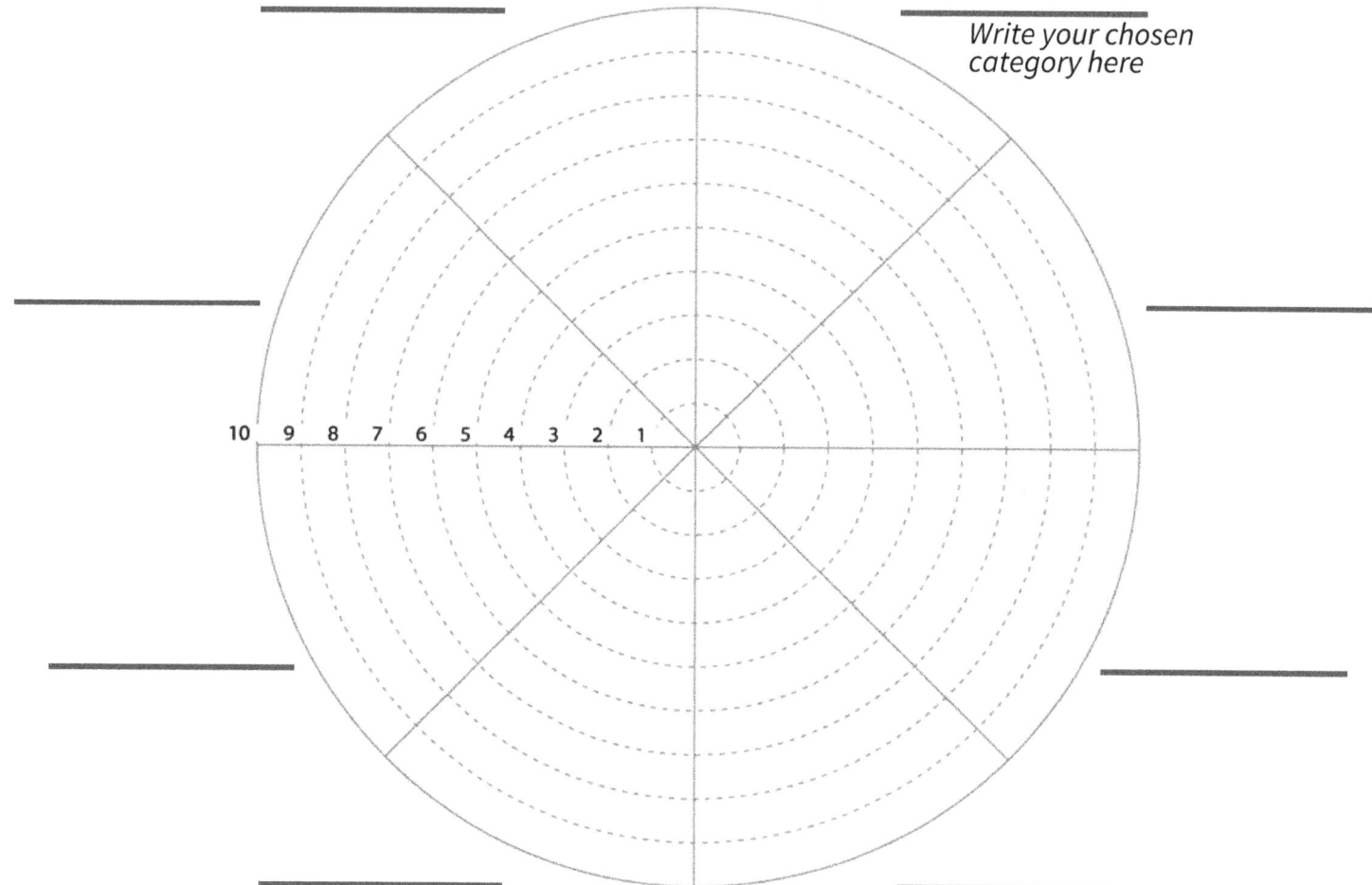

*Write your chosen category here*

**Once you're done,** take time to review each individual segment to determine *why* you reflected that result. Is the result due to your conscious choice or is it the result of unconscious choices of self or possibly opinions and beliefs created by others? Use the energy of the Moon and the Universe to help you surrender and release what no longer serves you whilst attracting all that serves your highest good and the highest good for all.

Date:

# THE FIRST
# DESIRES ROAD MAP

Use this space to journal any insights you received from completing your Life Balance Wheel. Your insights become your desires road map.

 ## NOW YOU'RE READY TO MOONIFEST!

Now that you know what is working well and what may need more focus, love and inspired action, you can start to create a new vision for your life. As you move through the lunar phases, keep in mind your Desires Road Map as it's a way of viewing where you are and where you want to be.

When the next New Moon arrives, you can start Moonifesting! **Go to the 'Let the Moonifesting Begin' section of this journal to begin your journey.**

Date:

# THE SECOND
# DESIRES ROAD MAP

## MY LIFE BALANCE WHEEL

**You represent the centre of the wheel** and each segment represents each category of your life here on Earth – *as a spiritual being having a physical experience.* Add your categories to each segment and using a scale of 0 - 10 (0 = unfulfilled, 10 = completely fulfilled) colour in how fulfilled, happy and satisfied you are.

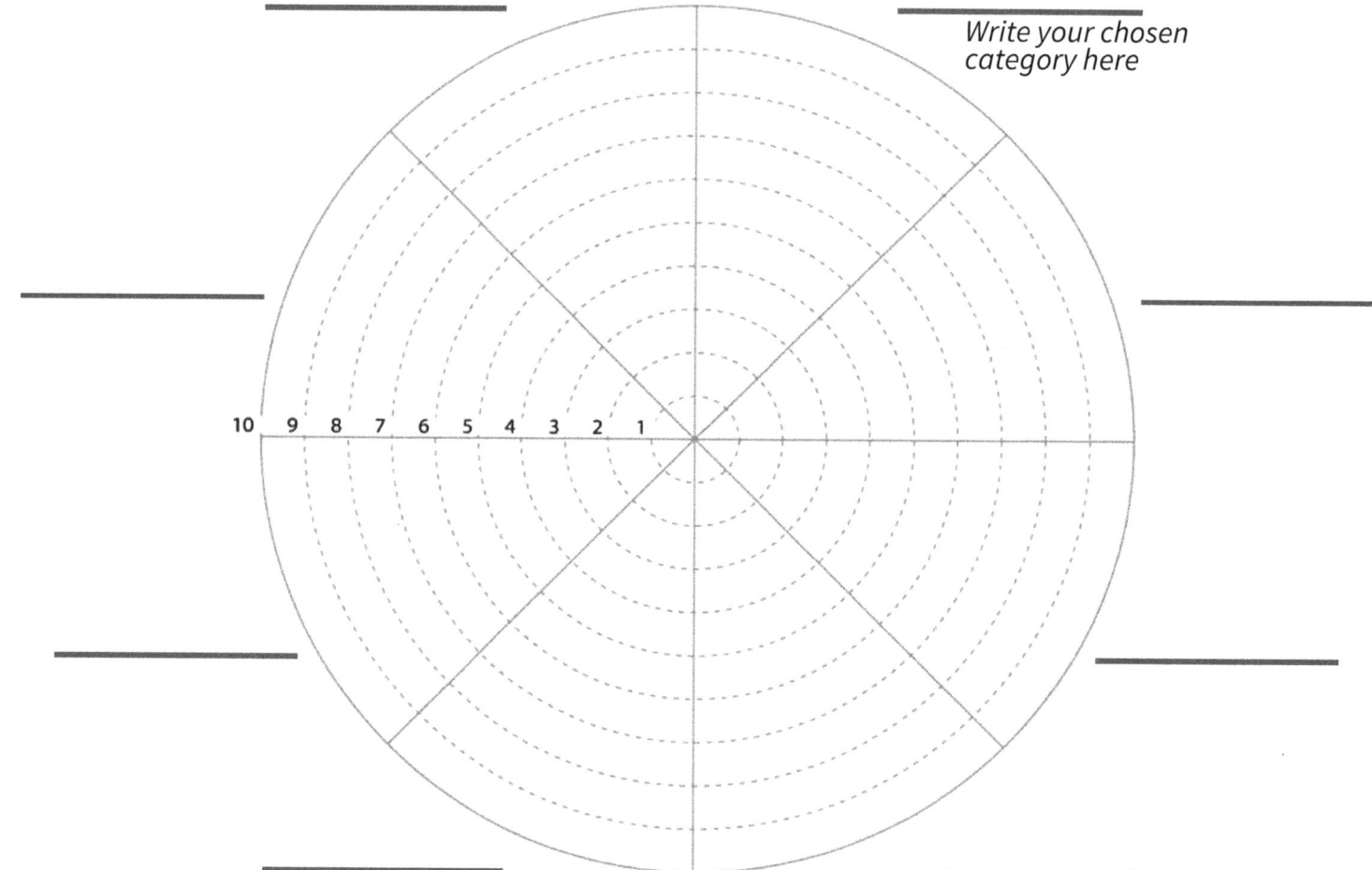

*Write your chosen category here*

**Once you're done,** take time to review each individual segment to determine *why* you reflected that result. Is the result due to your conscious choice or is it the result of unconscious choices of self or possibly opinions and beliefs created by others? Use the energy of the Moon and the Universe to help you surrender and release what no longer serves you whilst attracting all that serves your highest good and the highest good for all.

Date:

# THE SECOND DESIRES ROAD MAP

Use this space to journal any insights you received from completing your Life Balance Wheel. Your insights become your desires road map.

 ## NOW YOU'RE READY TO MOONIFEST!

Now that you know what is working well and what may need more focus, love and inspired action, you can start to create a new vision for your life. As you move through the lunar phases, keep in mind your Desires Road Map as it's a way of viewing where you are and where you want to be.

When the next New Moon arrives, you can start Moonifesting! **Go to the next New Moon within the 'Let the Moonifesting Begin' section of this book to continue your journey.**

Date:

# THE THIRD
# DESIRES ROAD MAP

## MY LIFE BALANCE WHEEL

**You represent the centre of the wheel** and each segment represents each category of your life here on Earth – *as a spiritual being having a physical experience.* Add your categories to each segment and using a scale of 0 - 10 (0 = unfulfilled, 10 = completely fulfilled) colour in how fulfilled, happy and satisfied you are.

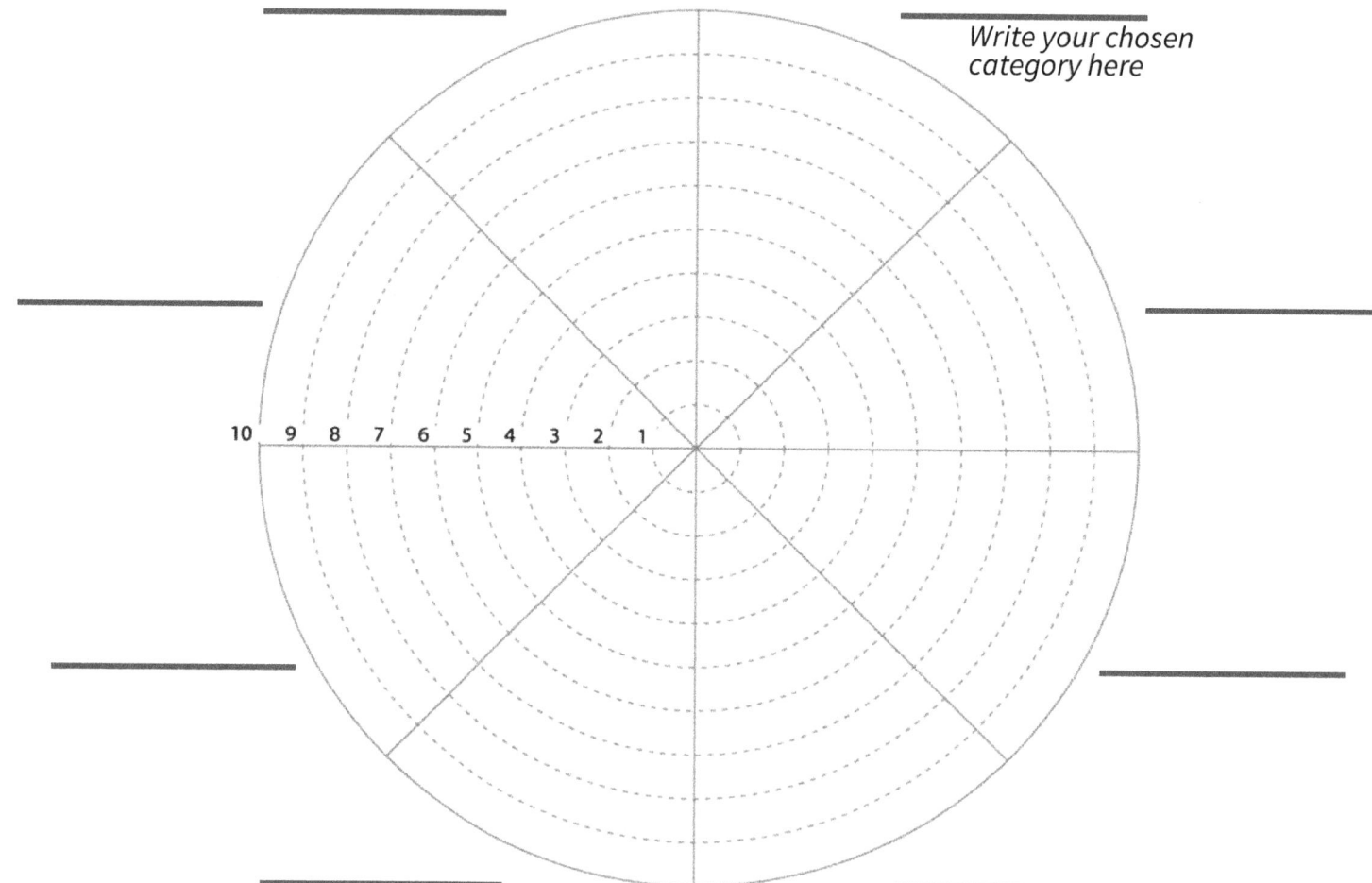

*Write your chosen category here*

**Once you're done,** take time to review each individual segment to determine *why* you reflected that result. Is the result due to your conscious choice or is it the result of unconscious choices of self or possibly opinions and beliefs created by others? Use the energy of the Moon and the Universe to help you surrender and release what no longer serves you whilst attracting all that serves your highest good and the highest good for all.

Date:

# THE THIRD
# DESIRES ROAD MAP

Use this space to journal any insights you received from completing your Life Balance Wheel. Your insights become your desires road map.

 ## NOW YOU'RE READY TO MOONIFEST!

Now that you know what is working well and what may need more focus, love and inspired action, you can start to create a new vision for your life. As you move through the lunar phases, keep in mind your Desires Road Map as it's a way of viewing where you are and where you want to be.

When the next New Moon arrives, you can start Moonifesting! **Go to the next New Moon within the 'Let the Moonifesting Begin' section of this book to continue your journey.**

# WELCOME TO *Moonifesting*

Welcome to the beginning of Moonifesting! This is where you'll be dreaming big, crushing through any obstacles, and reaching your goals. Here's a quick run down of what you can expect over the next lunar cycle and beyond.

Before you dive right in make sure you have done the following:

- Lovingly completed your **Moon Phase Calendar** so that you know when each of the Moon phases will occur depending on your geographic location. You'll be visiting your Moon Phase Calendar fairly regularly.
- Filled out your **Self Care Agreement** + signed and dated to keep you accountable.
- Completed the **First Desires Road Map** so you have a clear vision of what you're wanting to manifest into your life right now.

Over the page you'll find the **Lunar Cycle Plan**. This acts as a sort of monthly log to view your schedule, appointments and overall intentions. The difference is that we're working with the lunar dates not monthly dates. So the lunar cycle starts on the *first day of the New Moon and ends on the last day of the Waning Crescent.* The plan also has a habit tracker and mood tracker to give you some insight into how well you're reaching your goals and how you're feeling about life on a day-to-day basis. The beauty of this is that you decide what you want to include in your plan.

Following on from that are all the Moon phases of the lunar cycle (8 lunar phases in total). When the New Moon appears in your geographic location (refer to your Moon Phase Calendar for the date of when that will be) you'll officially start working with the energy of the New Moon. Then a few days after, you'll move onto the Waxing Crescent Moon phase of this journal and so on until you have completed all 8 lunar phases. Being that it's a cycle, you will then start again with a New Moon. This is why before every New Moon, you'll find a new Lunar Cycle Plan where you can record your schedule, appointments etc.

*Note:* It's important you don't skip ahead to other Moon phases because the energy of your intentions mightn't be in sync with the energy of the Moon. Remember that the idea of this book is to align your life with the natural rhythms of the Moon, so relax and let go. The Universe has got your back!

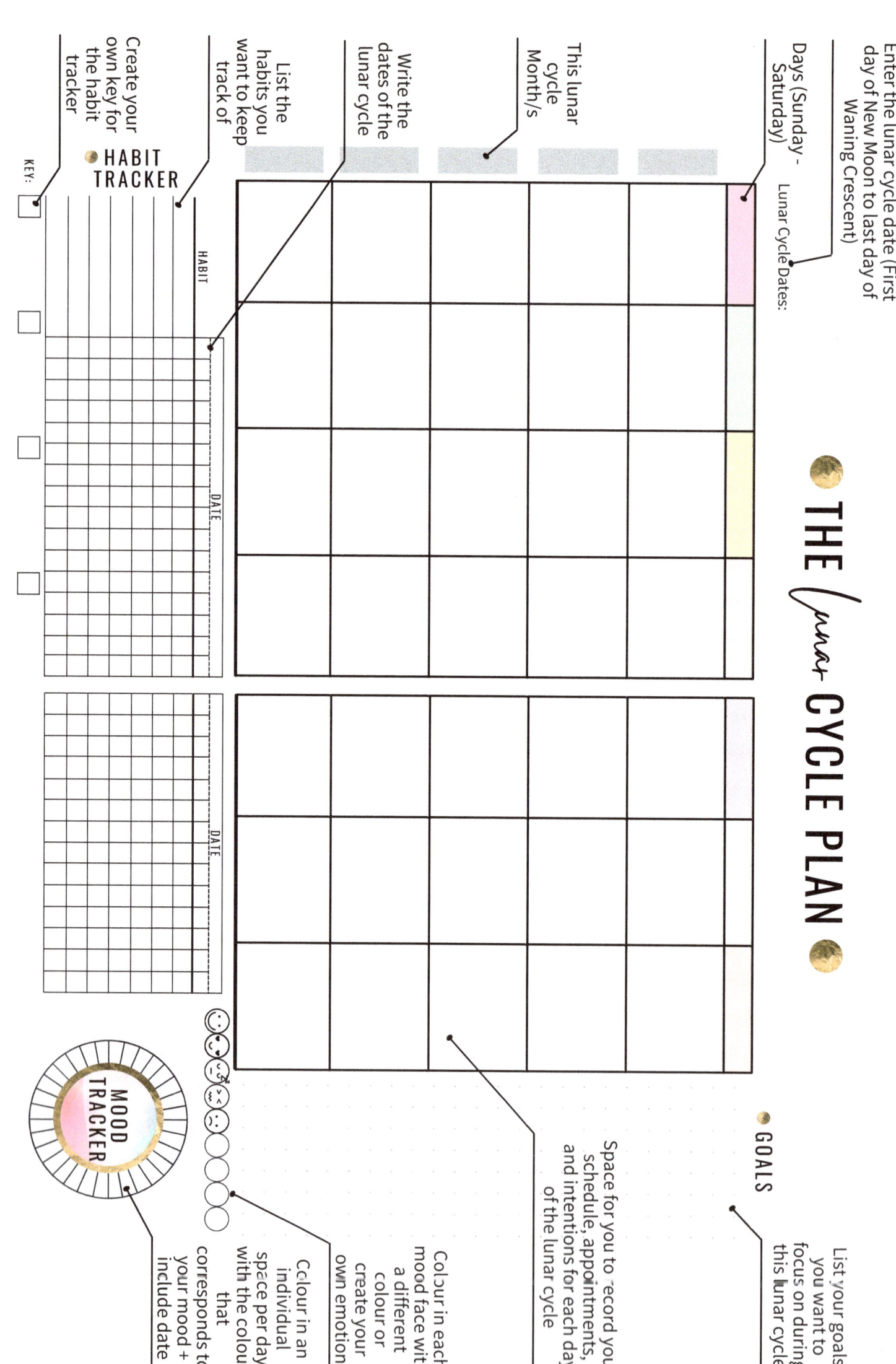

# THE lunar CYCLE PLAN

**Lunar Cycle Dates:** 10th June to 9th July

### 1

|  | MONDAY | TUESDAY | WEDNESDAY | THURSDAY | FRIDAY | SATURDAY | SUNDAY |
|---|---|---|---|---|---|---|---|
| June |  |  | JUNE | 10 ● New Moon<br>DAY OFF! | 11<br>DAY OFF | 12 Family BBQ | 13 $ Budget checkup |
| June | 14 | 15 ♡ Paint supply sourcing | 16 ★ 1 hour to myself<br>WORK | 17 School appt. @ 3:25pm | 18 👕 Passive Income Brainstorm | 19 ☀ Dinner @ 7pm | 20 $ Take kids to pool |
| June | 21 Kids play date @ 3:30pm | 22 | 23 Dental Appointment @ 3:00pm<br>WORK | 24 👕 First drawer | 25 ☀ Full Moon<br>Moon circle @ home 7:30pm | 26 ★ Chill Out!! | 27 $ Family Bushwalk |
| June/July | 28 👕 Second drawer | 29 | 30 ♡ Watch Paint landscape video<br>JULY<br>WORK | 1 Afternoon bushwalk | 2 ★ Meditate Class @ 6:00pm | 3 👕 Drop off clothes to charity | 4 ☀ $ Movie night! |
| July | 5 | 6 👕 Third drawer<br>WORK | 7 ★ Yoga @ 10am<br>DAY OFF! | 8 👕 Brainstorm Passive income - finalise<br>WORK | 9 ♡ Painting class @ 5:30pm |  |  |

### 2 GOALS

- $ Budget
- ♡ Learn to paint a landscape
- ★ Relaxation / me time
- 👕 Declutter wardrobe
- ☀ Date night (at least 2 this cycle)
- 👕 Create passive income - ideas brainstorm

### 3 HABIT TRACKER

| HABIT | 10 | 11 | 12 | 13 | 14 | 15 | 16 | 17 | 18 | 19 | 20 | 21 | 22 | 23 | 24 | 25 | 26 | 27 | 28 | 29 | 30 | 1 | 2 | 3 | 4 | 5 | 6 | 7 | 8 | 9 |
|---|---|---|---|---|---|---|---|---|---|---|---|---|---|---|---|---|---|---|---|---|---|---|---|---|---|---|---|---|---|---|
| Meditate | | | | | | | | | | | | | | | | | | | | | | | | | | | | | | |
| No junk food | | | ✕ | | | | | | | | | | | | | | | | | | | | | | | | | | | |
| 8+ hours of sleep | | | | | | | | | | | | | | | | | | | | | | | | | | | | | | |
| Stick to budget | | | | | | | | | ✕ | | | | | | | | | | | | | | | | | | | | | |
| Exercise 30+ minutes | | | | | | | | | | | | | | | | | | | | | | | | | | | | | | |
| Drink 2.7+ litres H₂O | | | | | | | | | | | | | | | | | | | | | | | | | | | | | | |
| Do something fun | | | | | | | | | | | | | | | | | | | | | | | | | | | | | | |

**KEY:** ✕ Habit free (planned) | ▨ Completed | ▧ Half Completed | ☐ Not able to complete

### 4 MOOD TRACKER

---

### 1 Lunar Cycle Plan:
Much like a monthly plan but instead focuses on the lunar cycle. The lunar cycle starts on the **first day of the New Moon and finishes on the last day of the Waning Crescent**. This plan gives you a birds eye view of your schedule, appointments, and intentions. Simply add the days of the week on the first row, the month name in each of the greyed areas of the first column, and the date in each of the boxes.

### 2 Goals:
Organise and prioritise your tasks and goals to encourage a healthy balance between fulfilling everyday life responsibilities and reaching your ultimate dreams. When the Waxing Crescent Moon phase comes around, you may like to add the goals that you decided to work on to the Lunar Cycle Plan.

### 3 Habit Tracker:
Decide on the habit you'd like to be kept accountable for and list them in the space provided. Then when you've completed the habit per day, you can mark it off. This helps you physically see the progress you're making and fuels you with motivation to keep going. It also breaks your bigger goals into smaller, day-by-day chunks, which helps you accomplish what you're aiming for in the long run. Remember to celebrate when you've stuck with your habit at the end of the lunar cycle!

### 4 Mood Tracker:
Keep track of your most-felt feeling each day so you can connect to your feelings and gain a better understanding of your triggers. In time you may even see a certain pattern emerge which can provide insight into what is working well in your life and what may need some more focus and self love.

Lunar Cycle Dates:

**HABIT TRACKER**

| HABIT | DATE |

KEY:

# CYCLE PLAN

## GOALS

DATE

MOOD TRACKER

Date:

# NEW MOON

New Beginnings | Unlimited Possibilities | Seeds of Intention

This is the perfect time to gather all your intentions and release them to the Universe. So spend some quiet time during the New Moon and explore the Desire Question:

## 'IF I COULD BE ANYTHING, DO ANYTHING, AND HAVE ANYTHING, WHAT WOULD IT BE?'

On the next page write a list, journal, or draw every single thing that comes to mind no matter how far-fetched it may seem. Try not to give into any thoughts that may tell you why you *can't* have what you desire. The world is your oyster! To further help you discover what your desires are, make sure you check in with your **First Desires Road Map** (found in the Desires Road Map section) which will help you define where there are imbalances in your life. These imbalances serve as beacons for what it is your soul is truly wanting.

And if that's not enough, there is also the Be, Do and Have questions below that you can answer if you feel a bit stuck. These questions are a great way to get the creative juices flowing.

| BE | DO | HAVE |
|---|---|---|
| Who do I aspire to be and why? | What are 5 things I love to do that bring me joy? | What is my ideal health level? |
| What are the top 3 things I would like to be? (e.g. chef, florist, author etc) | If I had no commitments, how would I spend my days? | If money were no object, what tangible things would be in my life? |
| What are the most important things to me right now and why? | What are 3 big things I'd love to accomplish this year and why? | If I had $50,000 who would I give it to and why? |
| How do I want to feel right now? | When the final curtain closes, what would I regret not having done whilst I was still living? | What kind of world do I want to live in? |

Date:

# NEW MOON
My Ultimate Wish List / Desires

## 'IF I COULD BE ANYTHING, DO ANYTHING, AND HAVE ANYTHING, WHAT WOULD IT BE?'

Consider the Desire Question above whilst keeping in mind the results of your First Desires Road Map. Now go ahead and make a list, journal, or draw all that you dream of. You can even stick inspirational cutouts from magazines and newspapers here too.

I am giving and receiving freely and generously, with an open heart and open mind

MOONIFESTING

Date:

# NEW MOON
My Ultimate Wish List / Desires

'IF I COULD BE ANYTHING, DO ANYTHING, AND HAVE ANYTHING, WHAT WOULD IT BE?'

*And so it is*

Date:

# NEW MOON
*Oracle Card Spread*

Record your New Moon oracle spread here (if you feel called to do one) and then consider how you could apply the messages you received to this lunar cycle and beyond.

Date:

# WAXING CRESCENT

Focus | Intention | Motivation | Curiosity

It's time to prioritise and refine your desires. Look at your wish list from the New Moon and categorise each desire into a realistic time period for when they may be achieved. Realise that the timeframe isn't set in stone but it can certainly help you decide on where your focus can be and what you intend to invest your energy on for the rest of the lunar cycle.

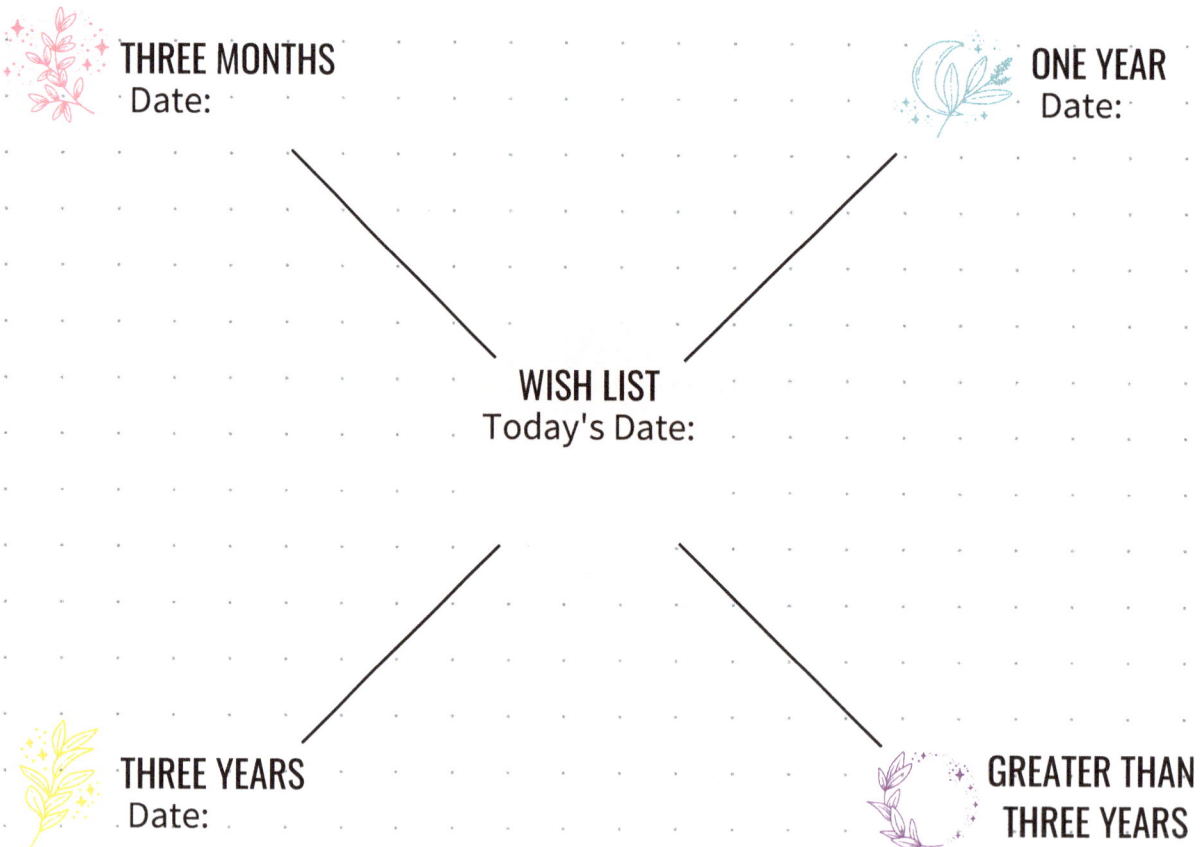

Now circle *one* desire from each timeframe (three months, one year, etc) that would have the most POSITIVE impact on YOUR LIFE and the LIVES OF OTHERS.

Date:

# WAXING CRESCENT

Focus | Intention | Motivation | Curiosity

From the desires you have circled on the previous page, answer the following questions:

Which desire will bring me the **most positive impact** to my life and the lives of others RIGHT NOW?

How do I want to **feel** during this lunar cycle and which desire journey would create that same feeling?

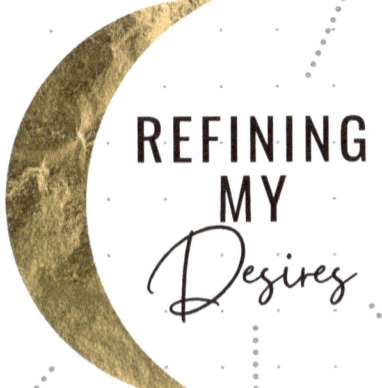

REFINING MY *Desires*

My **heart** tells me I should choose the following desire to achieve...

My **mind** tells me I should choose the following desire to achieve...

Will I follow my **heart** or **mind**?

MOONIFESTING

Date:

# WAXING CRESCENT

From your previous answers, which desire have you decided to focus on for the rest of this lunar cycle? If you have decided to work on more than one desire, make sure you're not overloading yourself with multiple tasks. Have confidence in your direction. You can achieve anything!

### The desire I have chosen
*to focus on during this lunar cycle is...*

*Because...*
*This your powerful motivator!*

*Affirmation*
I am receiving abundance now in expected and unexpected ways

Date:

# WAXING CRESCENT

*This or something better...*

Journal or draw how you picture your desire to be when it manifests into your life. Write in present-tense as if it has already happened. Include as much detail as possible such as how you feel and what you see, hear, smell, and taste.

## Inspiration

Become receptive of your thoughts. They're the beginning of what you create. If your thoughts focus on negativity, then your life will simulate that. Watch your thoughts and change the negative thoughts into loving and encouraging ones.

MOONIFESTING

Date:

# WAXING CRESCENT
*This or something better...*

## Manifestation Activity

Come back to these pages every day and view or read what you have written to remind yourself of your intention. Or spend 5 minutes a day visualising in your mind's eye your desire coming to fruition (this is a powerful manifestation practice!).

# MEDITATION FOR
## Manifestation

Set yourself a timer for at least 5 minutes and then get yourself very comfortable. Take a few deep breaths to centre yourself and let your eyelids close. As you inhale, fill up your lungs and your heart with your cleansing breath, and as you exhale, breathe into those spaces that are ready to receive new blessings, opportunities and joy. Keep doing this for a few moments.

Now bring your focus and thoughts onto what you want to call in - your deepest desire; the very thing or experience that you're ready to receive. And just imagine in this moment that you have already received this desire; already living it. You already know what it feels like to have it in your life. You can already see it and you may be able to touch it, smell it, and hear it. And so over the new few moments, simply focus on what your life looks like now that this desire has taken form. Just allow yourself to see what you see, feel what you feel, and hear what you hear. And if appropriate, you may even smell or taste something that relates to your desire coming into form. Maintain your focus on this special moment - play it through your mind, body and spirit as if it's already in your life, because it's already on it's way to you since you're a becoming a vibrational match to it. So by inviting all your senses into this meditation, you are essentially raising your vibration to match your desire. Continue this meditative practice until the timer ends.

Then ever so gently, open your eyes, move your body, take a deep breath and return to your day.

*Repeat this practice as often as needed to raise your vibration to match your desire.*

Date:

# FIRST QUARTER

Flexibility | Challenges | Decisions | Action

It's time to take inspired action yet often self doubt, anxieties and fears appear which can ultimately stop you from moving forward. Use this space to write or draw all that you're afraid of or all the possible setbacks you believe could happen when it comes to fulfilling your chosen desire. Trust that the Universe has your back and will support you on your path. If obstacles arise, you have the power to take bold steps for positive changes.

*Journal Prompt*

What are my usual excuses for why I don't have what I want? How can I change these excuses so they no longer affect me?

Date:

# FIRST QUARTER
*Journaling Opportunity*

## Self Love Reminder

Celebrate your uniqueness and weirdness, and the world will too. Because the words you use to describe yourself, the actions you take to look after yourself, and the choices you make to express yourself, all show the world who you are – that you are a one-of-a-kind creation that deserves their place on this planet. Own it and live it!

Date:

# FIRST QUARTER (AND BEYOND)
## *Desire Related Tasks*

Now is the perfect time to schedule out the smaller tasks which get you closer to your larger goal (desire). Write down all the necessary tasks you sense are needed to achieve your desire / goal. If you're unsure what tasks to take ask the Universe for a sign or do an oracle card reading for clarity and guidance. You don't need to know *all* the tasks, just enough to get started. And remember; sometimes the unexpected can happen so it's important to be open to make changes if needed. These changes can be made anytime during the Lunar cycle and beyond.

**EXAMPLE:**
Create a vision board to reflect my desire

**MY DESIRE / GOAL:**

Realistic Due date:

**TO DO NEXT...**
Number all the tasks in order so you end up with a sequential timeline

# FIRST QUARTER (AND BEYOND)

*Action Plan*

Date:

Now select the **first 3 tasks** and write down, in sequential order, the detailed steps (e.g. what you need, how many, who to contact etc.) and resources needed to achieve each task. Next, add a realistic timeframe of when you expect to have each step completed taking into account other life responsibilities. **Then actively DO THEM!** Once a step has been achieved, tick it off and celebrate! Any changes that need to be made to the steps can be completed in the Changes column which you can do anytime throughout the Lunar cycle.

| | TASK | STEPS | RESOURCES | DUE | CHANGES | DONE |
|---|---|---|---|---|---|---|
| **INFO** | What is the task you need to complete to fulfill your desire? | What steps do you need to take to complete the task? | What resources will you need including material items, personal skills, and other people's involvement? | When can this step/s be realistically completed? | As you monitor your progress throughout the lunar cycle, are there any changes that may need to be made to the plan? | Tick each step once you have completed it and remember to CELEBRATE! |
| **EXAMPLE** | Create a vision board to reflect my desire | Cut out images from my magazines. Include powerful affirmations that inspire me. Create vision board with lots of glitter and stick vision board on my wall next to my bed | Cardboard + glue + pencils + stickers + magazines + glitter. | 11th Nov | | |
| | | Look at my vision board and meditate on how it would look, feel and sound. | | 6:30am everyday | | ✓ |

MOONIFESTING

Date:

# FIRST QUARTER (AND BEYOND)
*Action Plan*

| TASK | STEPS | RESOURCES | DUE | CHANGES | DONE |
|------|-------|-----------|-----|---------|------|
|      |       |           |     |         |      |
|      |       |           |     |         |      |
|      |       |           |     |         |      |
|      |       |           |     |         |      |
|      |       |           |     |         |      |

# FIRST QUARTER (AND BEYOND)
*Action Plan*

Date:

| TASK | STEPS | RESOURCES | DUE | CHANGES | DONE |
|------|-------|-----------|-----|---------|------|
|      |       |           |     |         |      |

EACH DAY IS FILLED WITH **INFINITE POTENTIAL** AND **POSSIBILITY** AND

*I am ready*

Date:

# WAXING GIBBOUS

REFINEMENT | REFOCUS | CHANGES | PATIENCE

Use this time to trust that your intentions will bear the fruits of your labour even if some changes may need to be made to the action plan. It might be hard to see how your efforts are paying off at this time, so it's important to keep track of how far you've come.

Use this space to journal how you're feeling about the progress of your plan and the journey you have travelled so far including any milestones (big or small) that you have achieved.

I choose to believe that all things are possible and I trust that I am always in the right place at every moment

Date:

# WAXING GIBBOUS
*This or something better...*

As you reflect on your progress so far whilst checking in with your inner guidance, are there any changes that need to be made to your action plan?

**Note: *If the changes still relate to your current plan,*** be sure to update the Changes column of your Action Plan found in the First Quarter of *this* Moon cycle.

***If the changes no longer relate to your current plan (which is completely okay!)*** then write or draw what your new plan is here and then complete the Refined Action Plan on the following page.

Date:

# WAXING GIBBOUS (AND BEYOND)
*Refined Action Plan*

Write down **3 tasks** you could easily complete for the duration of this current lunar cycle and the associated steps needed to achieve each task.
Rememer to tick off each one once they're done and celebrate your progress!

| TASK | STEPS | RESOURCES | DUE | DONE |
|------|-------|-----------|-----|------|
|      |       |           |     |      |

Date:

# FULL MOON

RELEASE SETBACKS | CELEBRATE | SELF-LOVE

With the illumination of the Full Moon, it's time to become aware of what needs to be seen and understood (Shadow Work) in order for you to let go of expectations and attachments to certain outcomes. It's also a perfect time to celebrate the abundance in your life and give yourself some much needed self love!

So let's get started! Just follow the simple questions and prompts in this Full Moon section. And as a gentle reminder, and if you haven't already, you may like to practice a specific Full Moon ritual (see *The Moon Ritual* section, particularly the *Quick Moon Ritual Guide Step-by-Step* section in this book which gives you all the information on how to do one) as a way of celebrating and releasing any setbacks with intention and care. Let's begin!

What does the word 'Happiness' mean to you? What does happiness look like in your life? (*Tip: Do more of this!*)

Finish this sentence (don't over think it, just answer it!): *I love who I am because…*

*Embrace your true nature gorgeous soul!*

Date:

# FULL MOON
*Oracle Card Spread*

Record your Full Moon oracle spread here (if you feel called to do one) and consider how the messages that you receive can be applied to where you are in life right now and where you're going.

MOONIFESTING

Date:

# FULL MOON
## Journaling Opportunity

"Yesterday is heavy. Put it down" - *Unknown*

Recalibrate your approval meter: Comparing yourself to others whether you do it to compete or to validate your worth is a natural habit but not necessarily the most uplifting one. Become aware of how often you look outwards and do things purely so others will like you; whether that be by the way you act, the clothes you wear, or how you spend your time. Then transfer your attention inwards. Ask yourself, what do *I want*? What do *I feel good doing*? How do *I want to show up every day*? It's time to be yourself super soul – there's no need for others to give you their approval!

Date:

# FULL MOON
## Shadow Work

Write a list or journal about all the things you're ready to let go of and why. You can also include those things that don't seem to relate to your overall plan. It's also a good idea to revisit the First Quarter section where you wrote about your fears and obstacles and consider if they're still relevant. The point is to just let it all out - don't hold back!

REMOVE THIS PAGE AND RIP IT UP OR BURN IT

Date:

# FULL MOON
## Shadow Work

REMOVE THIS PAGE AND RIP IT UP OR BURN IT

*I lovingly accept and release these shadows*

Hand on heart, do you acknowledge your part in this; that it is your choice to either let go of these shadows or hold onto them? If you ticked 'Yes', then sign and date below as a way of declaring your intention to accept, let these shadows go, and move on with confidence.

Yes  No

_____    _____
Your Signature                                    Date

When you feel ready, burn or rip up this page as a symbol of release and liberation. Know that you are free of this energy that no longer serves your highest good.

Date:

# FULL MOON
## Journaling Opportunity

Now that you have released your shadows, you may like to sit in quiet contemplation and write or draw any thoughts, ideas, or impressions here.

There are no blocks I cannot overcome

MOONIFESTING

Date:

# WANING GIBBOUS

GRATITUDE | GIVE BACK | LOVE FULLY

This is a time to give gratitude to the Universe for all that you have harvested and experienced so far on this journey of life.

Write down all the things you're grateful for (things, experiences, people, yourself etc). To add a burst of colour you could even colour each one in!

**I AM grateful for...**

- Fresh air and trees
- My morning herbal tea
- Unconditional Universal love

Date:

# WANING GIBBOUS
## Journaling Opportunity

Use this space to journal what has been revealed to you so far during this lunar cycle. With those revelations, you may like to consider what you'll do about them now, what you have learned so far, and how you can apply that to your intentions. It's also a good time to reflect on whether your goals are for the good of others as well as for yourself. And if things aren't turning out as planned, try to use your intuition to sense if you need to accept a different outcome.

Date:

# WANING GIBBOUS
## Journaling Opportunity

## Give Back

This is the perfect time to share your positive vibes with others. Refer to the Give Back page of this journal and do one or more of the suggested activities. Spread those high-vibes dear soul!

Date:

# THIRD QUARTER

RELEASE | LET GO | FORGIVENESS

Throughout the lunar cycle you may have been hurt, disappointed, broken or angered in different ways, so now is the time to let go of any pent up emotions and negative thoughts that cause suffering.

Reflect on this lunar cycle. Is there any negative energy you need to and want to let go of? What do you need (if anything) to bring balance to yourself? Journal about it here.

*Journal Prompt*

What does 'letting go' mean to you? Start by writing the words, 'Letting go' makes me think…..and makes me feel…'

MOONIFESTING

Date:

# THIRD QUARTER
## Journaling Opportunity

### Declutter Reminder

It's time to remove any distractions and excessive stress from your life. Refer to the Declutter portion of this book for ideas and inspiration on how to make space for the important things.

Date:

# THIRD QUARTER
*Prayer to the Universe*

Sit somewhere comfortably where you won't be distracted. Take a few deep breaths to centre yourself. When you're ready read the following prayer to yourself slowly with the intention that this prayer is being directed to your soul and the Universe. You might like to do this a number of times as you allow the words to sink into your psyche. Try to *feel* into what the words represent for you. Lastly, say the prayer aloud as many times as you wish before finishing it off with another deep and cleansing breath.

**Note:** If you do not resonate with this prayer, then you may like to write your own for this particular Third Quarter Moon phase.

*Dearest Universe,
I surrender my agendas, timelines, and desires to you.
I know I was trying to control my life's outcome, but now I realise that by placing my trust in you and in the infinite energy of limitless possibilities, that you will lead me towards solutions of the highest good for all. Thank you.*

*And so it is.*

*Notes:*

Date:

# WANING CRESCENT

SURRENDER | REFLECTION | REST & RESTORE

As you bring closure to this lunar cycle, now is the perfect time to honour and love your strengths, realisations and accomplishments.

Reflect on how far you have come. Journal all the ways you have grown and what you have learned over the past lunar cycle.

Return to nature. Leave technology behind and get out into nature. Nature is one of the best ways to lower stress and ease anxiety. The fresh air, natural sunlight, Vitamin D, and free aromatherapy does wonders for your soul. Sit outside or go a step further and walk barefoot on the ground. This is such a powerful grounding exercise that will help you absorb free electrons from the Earth which has a surprisingly powerful antioxidant effect on the body. Not to mention it's got to be better than sitting starring at a pixelated screen!

Date:

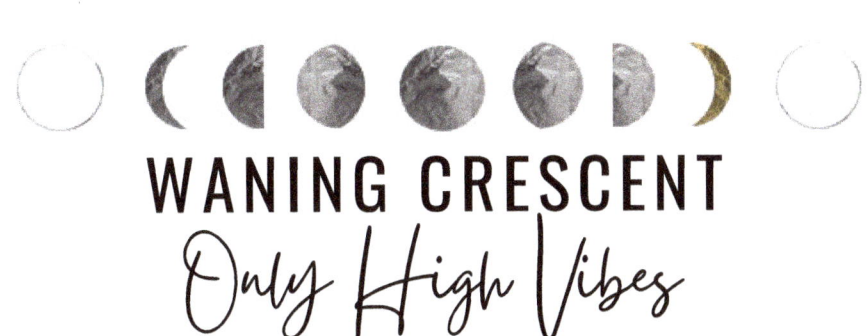

# WANING CRESCENT
## Only High Vibes

If you sense your mind, body, spirit is in need of a positive energy boost, write down what you could do to bring about those high vibes and then actively do them!

_____ _____ _____
*Mind* *Body* *Spirit*

In addition to that, take some time to let your mind, body, spirit rest as you get creative by colouring in this mandala.

MOONIFESTING

# THE *lunar*

Lunar Cycle Dates:

## HABIT TRACKER

| HABIT | DATE |

KEY:

# CYCLE PLAN

GOALS

DATE

MOOD TRACKER

Date:

# NEW MOON

New Beginnings | Unlimited Possibilities | Seeds of Intention

It's a New Moon which means a fresh start. Perhaps you're wanting to pick up from where you left off from the previous lunar cycle or maybe you're ready to set your focus and awareness on something entirely different. Either way, spend some quiet time exploring the Desire Question below whilst keeping in mind the results of your **First Desires Road Map** (found in the Desires Road map section of this journal) to create your ultimate wish list. Don't worry if the wish list is similar to the previous lunar cycle. The idea here is to just be in the moment, gather your intentions, and release them into the Universe.

## 'IF I COULD BE ANYTHING, DO ANYTHING, AND HAVE ANYTHING, WHAT WOULD IT BE?'

Remember; there's also the Be, Do and Have questions below that you can answer if you feel a bit stuck. These questions are a great way to get the creative juices flowing and open up the endless possibilities.

| BE | DO | HAVE |
|---|---|---|
| Who do I aspire to be and why? | What are 5 things I love to do that bring me joy? | What is my ideal health level? |
| What are the top 3 things I would like to be? (e.g. chef, florist, author etc) | If I had no commitments, how would I spend my days? | If money were no object, what tangible things would be in my life? |
| What are the most important things to me right now and why? | What are 3 big things I'd love to accomplish this year and why? | If I had $50,000 who would I give it to and why? |
| How do I want to feel right now? | When the final curtain closes, what would I regret not having done whilst I was still living? | What kind of world do I want to live in? |

Date:

# NEW MOON
My Ultimate Wish List / Desires

## 'IF I COULD BE ANYTHING, DO ANYTHING, AND HAVE ANYTHING, WHAT WOULD IT BE?'

Consider the Desire Question above whilst keeping in mind the results of your First Desires Road Map. Now go ahead and make a list, journal, or draw all that you dream of. You can even stick inspirational cutouts from magazines and newspapers here too.

I am co-creating my destiny with my inner wisdom and the Universe

MOONIFESTING

Date:

# NEW MOON
My Ultimate Wish List / Desires

**'IF I COULD BE ANYTHING, DO ANYTHING, AND HAVE ANYTHING, WHAT WOULD IT BE?'**

*And so it is*

Date:

# NEW MOON
## Oracle Card Spread

Record your New Moon oracle spread here (if you feel called to do one) and then consider how you could apply the messages you received to this lunar cycle and beyond.

Date:

# WAXING CRESCENT

Focus | Intention | Motivation | Curiosity

It's time to prioritise and refine your desires. Look at your wish list from the New Moon and categorise each desire into a realistic time period for when they may be achieved. Realise that the timeframe isn't set in stone but it can certainly help you decide on where your focus can be and what you intend to invest your energy on for the rest of the lunar cycle.

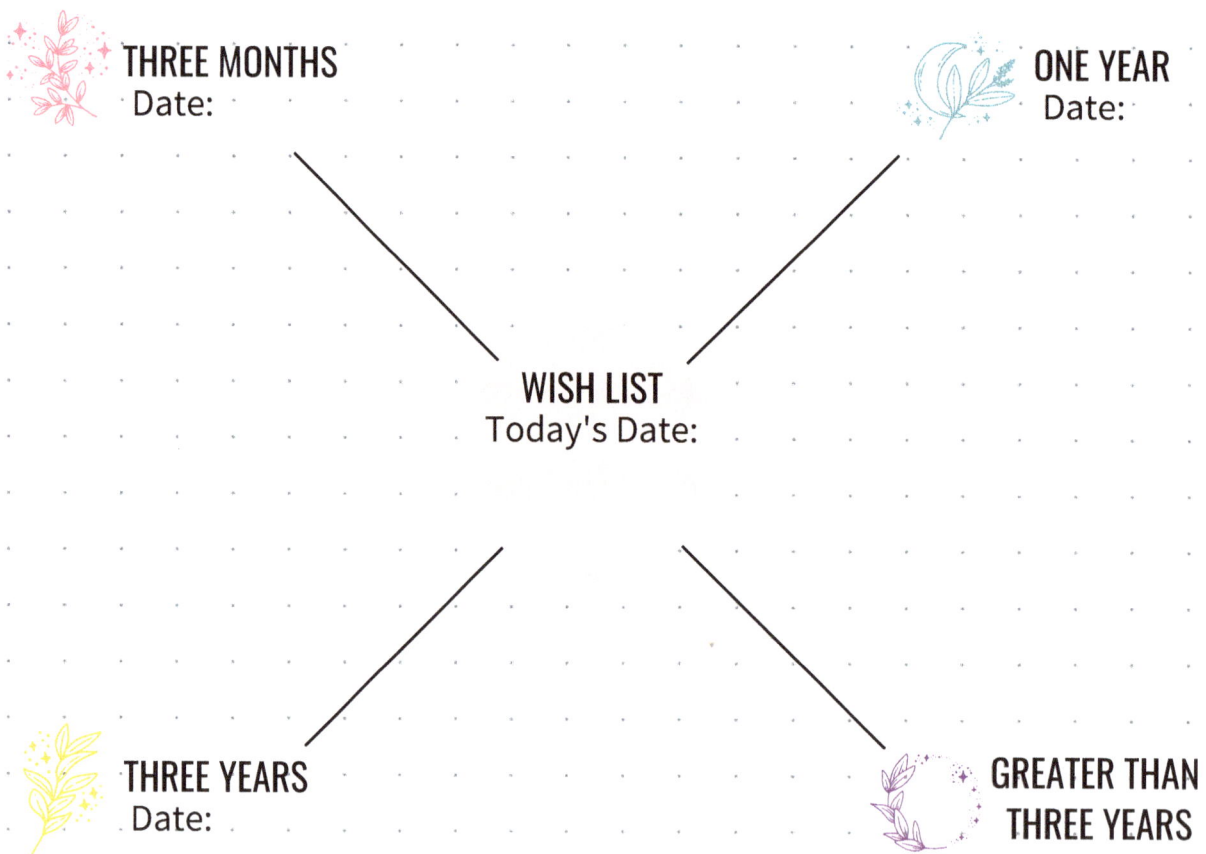

Now circle *one* desire from each timeframe (three months, one year, etc) that would have the most POSITIVE impact on YOUR LIFE and the LIVES OF OTHERS.

Date:

# WAXING CRESCENT

Focus | Intention | Motivation | Curiosity

From the desires you have circled on the previous page, answer the following questions:

*Which desire will bring me the **most positive impact** to my life and the lives of others RIGHT NOW?*

*How do I want to **feel** during this lunar cycle and which desire journey would create that same feeling?*

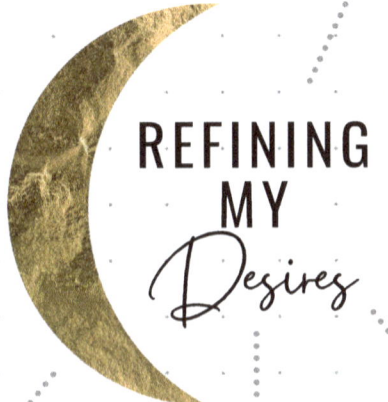

REFINING MY *Desires*

*My **heart** tells me I should choose the following desire to achieve...*

*My **mind** tells me I should choose the following desire to achieve...*

*Will I follow my **heart** or **mind** this time?*

MOONIFESTING

Date:

# WAXING CRESCENT

From your previous answers, which desire have you decided to focus on for the rest of this lunar cycle? If you have decided to work on more than one desire, make sure you're not overloading yourself with multiple tasks. Have confidence in your direction. You can achieve anything!

**The desire I have chosen**
*to focus on during this lunar cycle is...*

*Because...*
This your powerful motivator!

*Aha Moment*

Within you dwells the infinite wisdom of the sacred creative force of All that is, will be, and ever was – that's powerful stuff!

Date:

# WAXING CRESCENT

*This or something better...*

Journal or draw how you picture your desire to be when it manifests into your life. Write in present-tense as if it has already happened. Include as much detail as possible such as how you feel and what you see, hear, smell, and taste.

## TO DO...

Come back to this page every day to remind yourself of your intention or spend 5 minutes a day visualising in your mind's eye your desire coming to fruition (this is a powerful manifestation practice!).

## Inspiration

Expectation is everything. If you expect it will happen then it will, but if you expect it won't, then it won't. Be mindful of your expectation and if you secretly don't believe in your dreams then ask yourself, 'what stops me from believing?'

MOONIFESTING

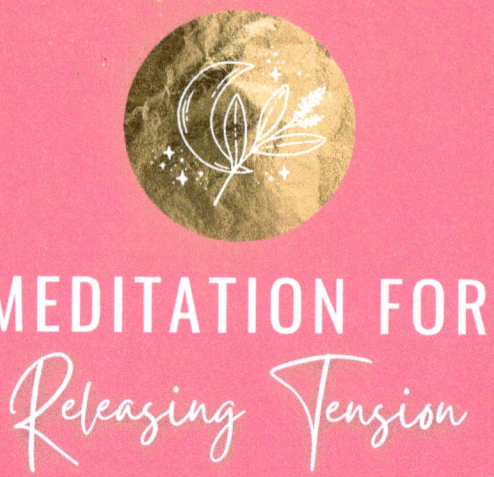

# MEDITATION FOR
## *Releasing Tension*

Close your eyes and relax. Take a few deep breaths from your diaphragm and release the tension in your body. Focus on a five-count breath where you'll be visualising your breath as a coloured light that represents healing and relaxation.

Slowly inhale from the stomach, then into ribs, then into chest, up into crown of the head and then gently hold the breath for the fifth count.

Reverse this process on the exhale for another count of five. Exhaling from the crown, chest, ribs, stomach and pausing on the last bit of breath before you breathe out completely.

As you continue to breathe this way, try to visualise your breath as a colour that represents healing and relaxation. So as you're breathing in, you can imagine that colour moving from your toes all the way up to the crown of your head, and as you breathe out, you can imagine any tension or stress leaving your body whether it be through your toes, escaping your entire body in all directions or just simply melting away.

Keep focusing on your breath while you imagine the healing and relaxed colour moving through your body whilst any stress or tension is released.

Do this for another 3 minutes and then return to your day.

Date:

# FIRST QUARTER

Flexibility | Challenges | Decisions | Action

Use this space to write or draw all that you're afraid of or all the possible setbacks you believe could happen when it comes to fulfilling your chosen desire. Remember: If obstacles arise, you have the power to take bold steps for positive changes!

*Journal Prompt*

What is the upside of staying where I am? What do I essentially avoid?

MOONIFESTING

Date:

# FIRST QUARTER
## Journaling Opportunity

### Self Love Reminder

Do you ever give great advice to others but fail to take your own advice? Many people do! So how can you get through to yourself? What needs to happen for you to stop and listen to your own inner wisdom and guidance? Invite your answer to be included in your life from now on.

Date:

# FIRST QUARTER (AND BEYOND)
## Desire Related Tasks

Now is the perfect time to schedule out the smaller tasks which get you closer to your larger goal. Write down all the necessary tasks you sense are needed to achieve your desire.

**If your desire / goal is still the same from the previous lunar cycle** then reflect on whether additional tasks may need to be assigned and write them here.

EXAMPLE:
Create a vision board to reflect my desire

### MY DESIRE / GOAL:

Realistic Due date:

## TO DO NEXT...
Number all the tasks in order so you end up with a sequential timeline

Date:

# FIRST QUARTER (AND BEYOND)
*Action Plan*

Now select the **first 3 tasks** and write down, in sequential order, the detailed steps (e.g. what you need, how many, who to contact etc.) and resources needed to achieve each task. Next, add a realistic timeframe of when you expect to have each step completed taking into account other life responsibilities. **Then actively DO THEM!** Once a step has been achieved, tick it off and celebrate! Any changes that need to be made to the steps can be completed in the Changes column which you can do anytime throughout the Lunar cycle.

## INFO

### TASK
What is the task you need to complete to fulfill your desire?

### STEPS
What steps do you need to take to complete the task?

### RESOURCES
What resources will you need including material items, personal skills, and other people's involvement?

### DUE
When can this step/s be realistically completed?

### CHANGES
As you monitor your progress throughout the lunar cycle, are there any changes that may need to be made to the plan?

### DONE
Tick each step once you have completed it and remember to CELEBRATE!

# FIRST QUARTER (AND BEYOND)
*Action Plan*

Date:

| TASK | STEPS | RESOURCES | DUE | CHANGES | DONE |
|------|-------|-----------|-----|---------|------|
|      |       |           |     |         |      |

Date:

# FIRST QUARTER (AND BEYOND)
*Action Plan*

| TASK | STEPS | RESOURCES | DUE | CHANGES | DONE |
|------|-------|-----------|-----|---------|------|
|      |       |           |     |         |      |
|      |       |           |     |         |      |
|      |       |           |     |         |      |
|      |       |           |     |         |      |

EVERY MORNING
I WAKE UP WITH
THOUGHTS
AND FEELINGS
THAT ARE
*Nourishing*

Date:

# WAXING GIBBOUS

REFINEMENT | REFOCUS | CHANGES | PATIENCE

Use this space to journal how you're feeling about the progress of your plan and the journey you have travelled so far including any milestones (big or small) that you have achieved.

*Affirmation*

I choose to believe that all things are possible and I trust that I am always in the right place at every moment

Date:

# WAXING GIBBOUS

*This or something better...*

As you reflect on your progress so far whilst checking in with your inner guidance, are there any changes that need to be made to your action plan?

**Note:** ***If the changes still relate to your current plan,*** be sure to update the Changes column of your Action Plan. Trust that your plan and support from the Universe will take you to the finish line.

***If the changes no longer relate to your current plan (which is completely okay!)*** then write or draw your new plan below and complete the Refined Action Plan on the following page.

Date:

# WAXING GIBBOUS (AND BEYOND)

*Refined Action Plan*

Write down **3 tasks** you could easily complete for the duration of this current lunar cycle and the associated steps needed to achieve each task. Remeber to tick off each one once they're done and celebrate your progress!

| TASK | STEPS | RESOURCES | DUE | DONE |
|------|-------|-----------|-----|------|
|      |       |           |     |      |
|      |       |           |     |      |
|      |       |           |     |      |

Date:

# WAXING GIBBOUS (AND BEYOND)
*Refined Action Plan*

Write down **3 tasks** you could easily complete for the duration of this current lunar cycle and the associated steps needed to achieve each task.
Remember to tick off each one once they're done and celebrate your progress!

| TASK | STEPS | RESOURCES | DUE | DONE |
|------|-------|-----------|-----|------|
|      |       |           |     |      |
|      |       |           |     |      |
|      |       |           |     |      |

MOONIFESTING

Date:

# FULL MOON

RELEASE SETBACKS | CELEBRATE | SELF-LOVE

It's time to become aware of what needs to be seen and understood (Shadow Work) in order to release any setbacks. It's also a time to celebrate your beautiful nature and the magical life you're leading. As a gentle reminder (and if you haven't already) you may like to practice a specific Full Moon ritual (see The Moon Ritual section, particularly the Quick Moon Ritual Guide Step-by-Step section in this book which gives you all the information on how to do one) as a way of maintaining focus and connecting with the Full Moon's energy. Are you ready to go? Let's begin!

What are the things that give you energy; the things or experiences that fill your well? *(Tip: Do these more often!)*

Finish this sentence (don't over think it, just answer it!): *I came into this world to...*

*Shine your light dear soul!*

Date:

# FULL MOON
## Oracle Card Spread

Record your Full Moon oracle spread here (if you feel called to do one) and consider how the messages that you receive can be applied to where you are in life right now and where you're going.

MOONIFESTING

Date:

# FULL MOON
## Journaling Opportunity

*"Feel appreciation for what is. And eagerness for what is coming"* – *Abraham Hicks*

## Self Love Reminder

Celebrate your screw ups: Mistakes are often seen as negative and shameful. At some point you were taught that you're not allowed to fall short of something and that it's better to avoid making a mistake at all costs. But today you're going to celebrate your mistakes knowing that it's okay (and normal) to be perfectly imperfect. Laugh at yourself, forgive yourself, and affirm that despite your mistakes, you're still okay. You mightn't always get it right or get what you want but you'll likely learn something that will bring you closer to your goals and an understanding of your true nature.

Date:

# FULL MOON
## Shadow Work

Write a list or journal about all the things you're ready to let go of and why. You can also include those things that don't seem to relate to your overall plan. It's also a good idea to revisit the First Quarter section where you wrote about your fears and obstacles and consider if they're still relevant. The point is to just let it all out - don't hold back!

REMOVE THIS PAGE AND RIP IT UP OR BURN IT

MOONIFESTING

Date:

# FULL MOON
## Shadow Work

REMOVE THIS PAGE AND RIP IT UP OR BURN IT

*I lovingly accept and release these shadows*

Hand on heart, do you acknowledge your part in this; that it is your choice to either let go of these shadows or hold onto them? If you ticked 'Yes', then sign and date below as a way of declaring your intention to accept, let these shadows go, and move on with confidence.

**Yes** ☐  **No** ☐

_____     _____
Your Signature                                                           Date

When you feel ready, burn or rip up this page as a symbol of release and liberation. Know that you are free of this energy that no longer serves your highest good.

Date:

# FULL MOON
## Journaling Opportunity

Now that you have released your shadows, you may like to sit in quiet contemplation and write or draw any thoughts, ideas, or impressions here.

I am done being the victim. Now I shape my life by shaping my inner world

Date:

# WANING GIBBOUS

GRATITUDE | GIVE BACK | LOVE FULLY

This is your gratitude tree where you can write down all the things you're grateful for on each circled leaf. If you're really feeling creative, why not colour each one in!

*I am grateful for...*

Date:

# WANING GIBBOUS
## Journaling Opportunity

Use this space to journal what has been revealed to you so far during this lunar cycle. With those revelations, you may like to consider what you'll do about them now, what you have learned so far, and how you can apply that to your intentions. It's also a good time to reflect on whether your goals are for the good of others as well as for yourself. And if things aren't turning out as planned, try to use your intuition to sense if you need to accept a different outcome.

Date:

# WANING GIBBOUS
*Journaling Opportunity*

This is the perfect time to share your positive vibes with others. Refer to the Give Back page of this Journal and do one or more of the suggested activities. Spread those high-vibes dear soul!

Date:

# THIRD QUARTER

RELEASE | LET GO | FORGIVENESS

Throughout the lunar cycle you may have been hurt, disappointed, broken or angered in different ways, so now is the time to let go of any pent up emotions and negative thoughts that cause suffering.

Reflect on this lunar cycle. Is there any negative energy you need to and want to let go of? What do you need (if anything) to bring balance to yourself? Journal about it here.

*Journal Prompt*

During this lunar cycle, did anything hold you back from moving forward including yourself? Why?

Date:

# THIRD QUARTER
## Journaling Opportunity

## Declutter Reminder
It's time to remove any distractions and excessive stress from your life. Refer to the Declutter portion of this book for ideas and inspiration on how to make space for the important things.

Date:

# THIRD QUARTER
## *Prayer to the Universe*

Sit somewhere comfortably where you won't be distracted. Take a few deep breaths to centre yourself. When you're ready read the following prayer to yourself slowly with the intention that this prayer is being directed to your soul and the Universe. You might like to do this a number of times as you allow the words to sink into your psyche. Try to *feel* into what the words represent for you. Lastly, say the prayer aloud as many times as you wish before finishing it off with another deep and cleansing breath.

**Note:** If you do not resonate with this prayer, then you may like to write your own for this particular Third Quarter Moon phase.

*When I consider my presence here on this planet – the reason for my being here, I connect to something far deeper than gaining material things. I see this as a chance for me to translate my beautiful soul; my divine nature, into a human experience. I see this as a way to shine my light and be the person I want to see in this world despite my past and any restrictions placed upon me. So every day, I will remember this and be grateful to experience this world in its entirety.*

*And so it is.*

Notes:

Date:

# WANING CRESCENT

SURRENDER | REFLECTION | REST & RESTORE

As you bring closure to this lunar cycle, now is the perfect time to honour and love your strengths, realisations and accomplishments.

Reflect on how far you have come. Journal all the ways you have grown and what you have learned over the past lunar cycle.

Dance like nobody's watching. No matter how uncoordinated or left-footed you believe you are, dancing can shake the tension and energetic blocks within the body. Turn on your favourite beats and let your body do the talking. Don't worry about how you look – it's not about the moves, it's about letting go and having fun.

Date:

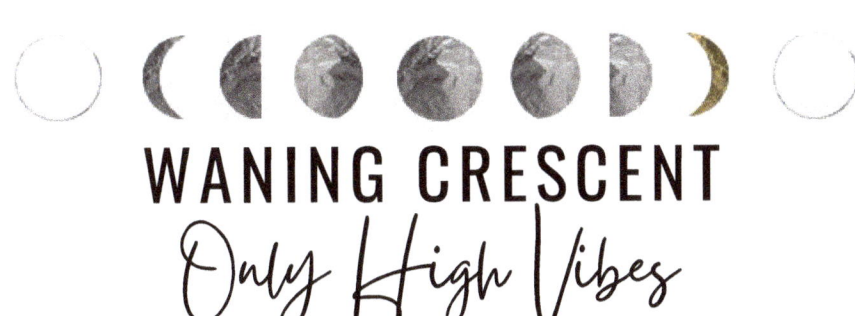

# WANING CRESCENT
*Only High Vibes*

If you sense your mind, body, spirit is in need of a positive energy boost, write down what you could do to bring about those high vibes and then actively do them!

_____    _____    _____
*Mind*    *Body*    *Spirit*

In addition to that, take some time to let your mind, body, spirit rest as you get creative by colouring in this mandala.

MOONIFESTING

# THE Lunar

Lunar Cycle Dates:

**HABIT TRACKER**

HABIT | DATE

KEY:

# CYCLE PLAN

Date:

# NEW MOON

New Beginnings | Unlimited Possibilities | Seeds of Intention

Welcome to the third New Moon of this journal! Congratulations on creating consistent momentum around Moonifesting! As always, this New Moon represents new beginnings, but instead of diving right in, go to the **Second Desires Road Map** (found in the Desires Road Map section of this journal) first and complete it to see how balanced and harmonious your life is right now. This will help you gauge where your soul wants to be and what your intentions are for this New Moon. Once you have done that come back here and continue working with the New Moon's energy.

## 'IF I COULD BE ANYTHING, DO ANYTHING, AND HAVE ANYTHING, WHAT WOULD IT BE?'

To create new intentions for this new lunar cycle, keep in mind the results of your Second Desires Road Map and the Desire Question above. You may even want to answer the Be, Do and Have questions below if you feel called to.

| BE | DO | HAVE |
|---|---|---|
| Who do I aspire to be and why? | What are 5 things I love to do that bring me joy? | What is my ideal health level? |
| What are the top 3 things I would like to be? (e.g. chef, florist, author etc) | If I had no commitments, how would I spend my days? | If money were no object, what tangible things would be in my life? |
| What are the most important things to me right now and why? | What are 3 big things I'd love to accomplish this year and why? | If I had $50,000 who would I give it to and why? |
| How do I want to feel right now? | When the final curtain closes, what would I regret not having done whilst I was still living? | What kind of world do I want to live in? |

Date:

# NEW MOON
My Ultimate Wish List / Desires

## 'IF I COULD BE ANYTHING, DO ANYTHING, AND HAVE ANYTHING, WHAT WOULD IT BE?'

Consider the Desire Question above whilst keeping in mind the results of your Second Desires Road Map. Now go ahead and make a list, journal, or draw all that you dream of. You can even stick inspirational cutouts from magazines and newspapers here too.

I am grateful for new challenges that help me grow and become stronger

Date:

# NEW MOON
My Ultimate Wish List / Desires

**'IF I COULD BE ANYTHING, DO ANYTHING, AND HAVE ANYTHING, WHAT WOULD IT BE?'**

*And so it is*

Date:

# NEW MOON
## Oracle Card Spread

Record your New Moon oracle spread here (if you feel called to do one) and then consider how you could apply the messages you received to this lunar cycle and beyond.

Date:

# WAXING CRESCENT

Focus | Intention | Motivation | Curiosity

It's time to prioritise and refine your desires. Look at your wish list from the New Moon and categorise each desire into a realistic time period for when they may be achieved. Realise that the timeframe isn't set in stone but it can certainly help you decide on where your focus can be and what you intend to invest your energy on for the rest of the lunar cycle.

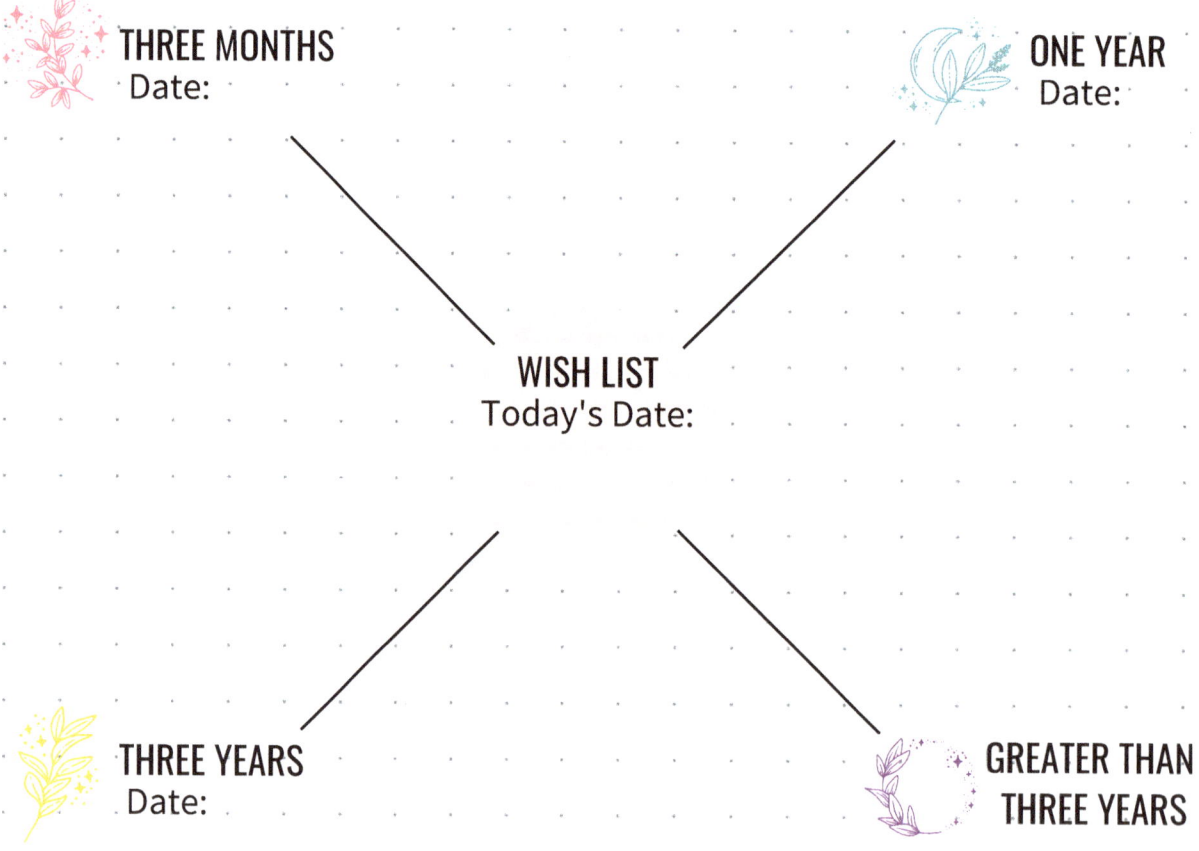

Now circle *one* desire from each timeframe (three months, one year, etc) that would have the most POSITIVE impact on YOUR LIFE and the LIVES OF OTHERS.

Date:

# WAXING CRESCENT

Focus | Intention | Motivation | Curiosity

From the desires you have circled on the previous page, answer the following questions:

*Which desire will bring me the **most positive impact** to my life and the lives of others RIGHT NOW?*

*How do I want to **feel** during this lunar cycle and which desire journey would create that same feeling?*

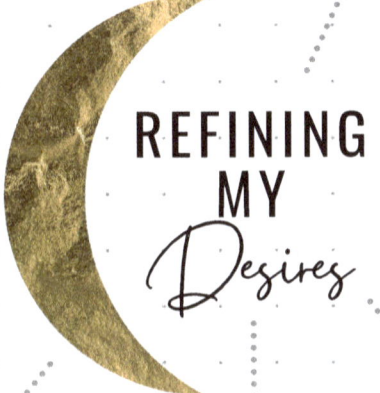

REFINING MY *Desires*

*My **heart** tells me I should choose the following desire to achieve...*

*My **mind** tells me I should choose the following desire to achieve...*

*Will I follow my **heart** or **mind** this time?*

MOONIFESTING

Date:

# WAXING CRESCENT

From your previous answers, which desire have you decided to focus on for the rest of this lunar cycle? If you have decided to work on more than one desire, make sure you're not overloading yourself with multiple tasks. Have confidence in your direction. You can achieve anything!

## The desire I have chosen
*to focus on during this lunar cycle is...*

## Because...
*This your powerful motivator!*

### Affirmation
I deserve a life of freedom and abundance – it's easy to create the life I desire

Date:

# WAXING CRESCENT

*This or something better...*

Journal or draw how you picture your desire to be when it manifests into your life. Write in present-tense as if it has already happened. Include as much detail as possible such as how you feel and what you see, hear, smell, and taste.

## TO DO...
Come back to this page every day to remind yourself of your intention or spend 5 minutes a day visualising in your mind's eye your desire coming to fruition (this is a powerful manifestation practice!).

### *Inspiration*
Avoid the naysayers who take pleasure in telling you their negative opinion about your dreams and desires. Instead, surround yourself around people who believe in you and will only lift you higher.

# MEDITATION MANTRA

Mantra is defined as a word or sound repeated to aid concentration in meditation. 'Man' means to think or the thinker and 'Tra' means tool or instrument. So Mantra is a tool for the thinker (the mind). The actual Mantra is a word or combination of words that are repeated 3, 6, 9, 27 and up to 108 times. Doing this keeps the mind clear of distracting thoughts whilst bringing calm and peace to the psyche.

**How to Do a Meditation Mantra:**

Sit comfortably in a chair or on the floor. Close your eyes and take a few slow deep breaths before returning to your natural breathing rate.

Repeat your mantra slowly and steadily out loud, concentrating on its sound as fully as you can. Repeat it in unison with the natural rhythm of your breath. You can split the mantra so you repeat half of it when you inhale and the other half when you exhale, or repeat the mantra on both the inhalation and the exhalation, or repeat it on exhalation only.

After about 10 recitations, repeat the mantra silently by moving only your lips (this helps you keep a steady pace). Then, after another 10 repetitions, recite it internally without moving your lips. As thoughts arise, simply return to the mantra; knowing this is a natural part of the process. Gently bring your attention back again and again, experiencing the internal sound as fully as possible.

Continue for the period of time you set aside for meditation. Then come out of the meditation by taking a few deep breaths and sitting quietly to sense what you feel.

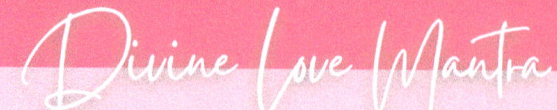

## Aham Prema (A-Hum Prey-Ma)

This mantra helps to calm your mind, body, soul. It's an excellent way to start your day and anytime youre feeling in need of love and connection.`

This translates to *"I am Divine Love"* making this a great mantra for anyone who is working on cultivating self-love. It also aligns and connects us to all of the love in the Universe.

Date:

# FIRST QUARTER

Flexibility | Challenges | Decisions | Action

Use this space to write or draw all that you're afraid of or all the possible setbacks you believe could happen when it comes to fulfilling your chosen desire. Remember: If obstacles arise, you have the power to take bold steps for positive changes!

*Journal Prompt*

What's my first memory of trying something new and it not working out. What happened? Am I willing to take a chance on myself to try something new despite my past experiences?

Date:

# FIRST QUARTER
## Journaling Opportunity

### Self Love Reminder

The next time you look in the mirror, say to your reflection, 'I love what I see – every little bit'. In time, you'll believe in those words and realise that there's nothing quite like the feeling of self love and appreciation to raise your vibration.

Date:

# FIRST QUARTER (AND BEYOND)
## *Desire Related Tasks*

Now is the perfect time to schedule out the smaller tasks which get you closer to your larger goal. Write down all the necessary tasks you sense are needed to achieve your desire.

**If your desire / goal is still the same from the previous lunar cycle** then reflect on whether additional tasks may need to be assigned and write them here.

EXAMPLE:
Create a vision board to reflect my desire

MY DESIRE / GOAL:

Realistic Due date:

## TO DO NEXT...
Number all the tasks in order so you end up with a sequential timeline

MOONIFESTING

Date:

# FIRST QUARTER (AND BEYOND)

*Action Plan*

Now select the **first 3 tasks** and write down, in sequential order, the detailed steps (e.g. what you need, how many, who to contact etc.) and resources needed to achieve each task. Next, add a realistic timeframe of when you expect to have each step completed taking into account other life responsibilities. **Then actively DO THEM!** Once a step has been achieved, tick it off and celebrate! Any changes that need to be made to the steps can be completed in the Changes column which you can do anytime throughout the Lunar cycle.

## INFO

| TASK | STEPS | RESOURCES | DUE | CHANGES | DONE |
|---|---|---|---|---|---|
| What is the task you need to complete to fulfill your desire? | What steps do you need to take to complete the task? | What resources will you need including material items, personal skills, and other people's involvement? | When can this step/s be realistically completed? | As you monitor your progress throughout the lunar cycle, are there any changes that may need to be made to the plan? | Tick each step once you have completed it and remember to CELEBRATE! |

# FIRST QUARTER (AND BEYOND)
*Action Plan*

Date:

| TASK | STEPS | RESOURCES | DUE | CHANGES | DONE |
|------|-------|-----------|-----|---------|------|
|      |       |           |     |         |      |

Date:

# FIRST QUARTER (AND BEYOND)
*Action Plan*

| TASK | STEPS | RESOURCES | DUE | CHANGES | DONE |
|------|-------|-----------|-----|---------|------|
|      |       |           |     |         |      |
|      |       |           |     |         |      |
|      |       |           |     |         |      |
|      |       |           |     |         |      |
|      |       |           |     |         |      |

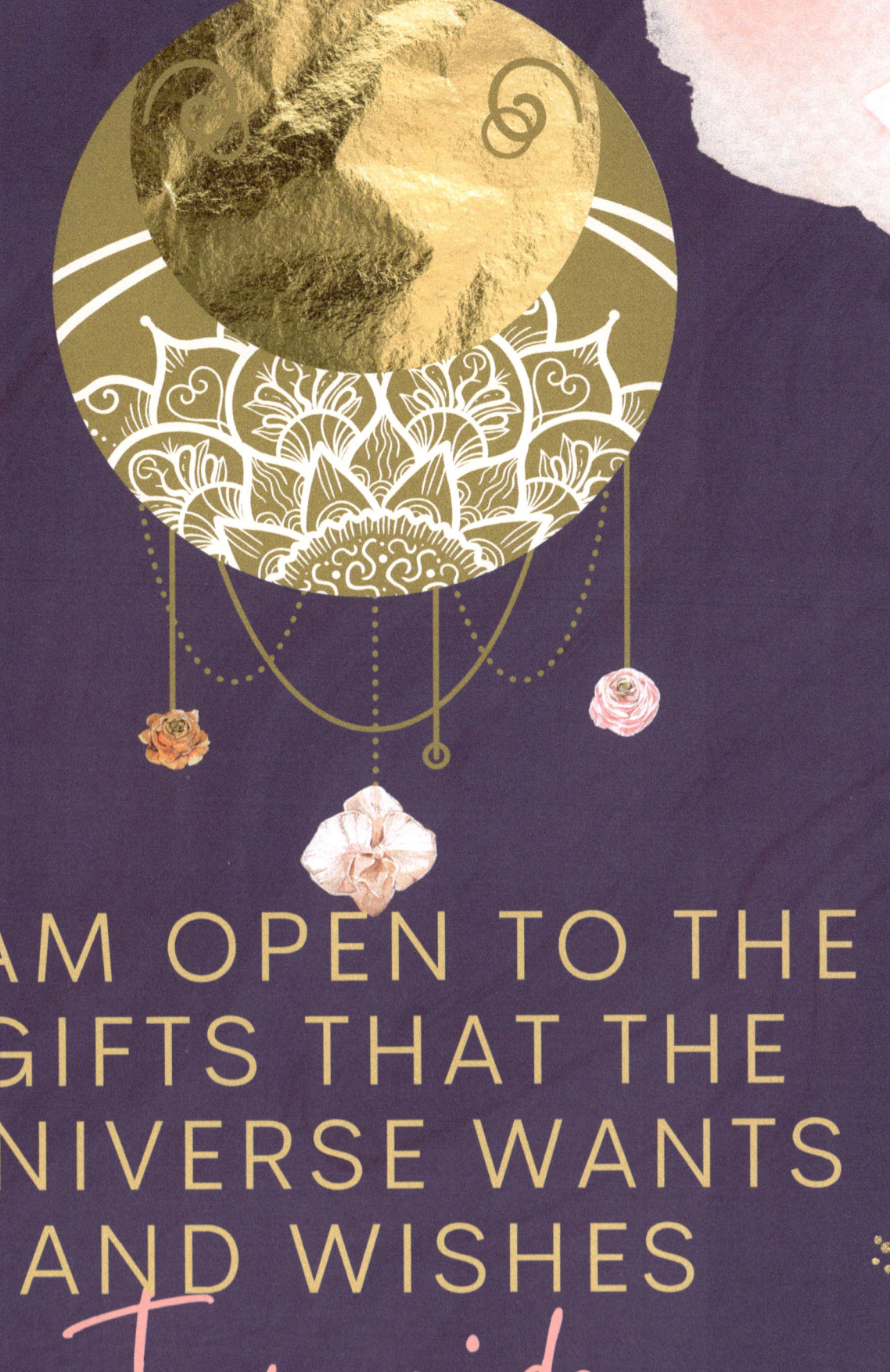

I AM OPEN TO THE GIFTS THAT THE UNIVERSE WANTS AND WISHES *To provide*

Date:

# WAXING GIBBOUS

REFINEMENT | REFOCUS | CHANGES | PATIENCE

Use this space to journal how you're feeling about the progress of your plan and the journey you have travelled so far including any milestones (big or small) that you have achieved.

*Affirmation*

I am completely aligned with the Universe and trust that everything happens for a reason

Date:

# WAXING GIBBOUS

*This or something better...*

As you reflect on your progress so far whilst checking in with your inner guidance, are there any changes that need to be made to your action plan?

**Note:** *If the changes still relate to your current plan*, be sure to update the Changes column of your Action Plan. Trust that your plan and support from the Universe will take you to the finish line.

*If the changes no longer relate to your current plan (which is completely okay!)* then write or draw your new plan below and complete the Refined Action Plan on the following page.

Date:

# WAXING GIBBOUS (AND BEYOND)
## Refined Action Plan

Write down **3 tasks** you could easily complete for the duration of this current lunar cycle and the associated steps needed to achieve each task. Remeber to tick off each one once they're done and celebrate your progress!

| TASK | STEPS | RESOURCES | DUE | DONE |
|------|-------|-----------|-----|------|
|      |       |           |     |      |
|      |       |           |     |      |
|      |       |           |     |      |

Date:

# WAXING GIBBOUS (AND BEYOND)
## Refined Action Plan

Write down **3 tasks** you could easily complete for the duration of this current lunar cycle and the associated steps needed to achieve each task. Rememer to tick off each one once they're done and celebrate your progress!

| TASK | STEPS | RESOURCES | DUE | DONE |
|------|-------|-----------|-----|------|
|      |       |           |     |      |

Date:

# FULL MOON

RELEASE SETBACKS | CELEBRATE | SELF-LOVE

It's time to become aware of what needs to be seen and understood (Shadow Work) in order to release any setbacks. It's also a time to celebrate your beautiful nature and the magical life you're leading. As a gentle reminder (and if you haven't already) you may like to practice a specific Full Moon ritual (see The Moon Ritual section, particularly the Quick Moon Ritual Guide Step-by-Step section in this book which gives you all the information on how to do one) as a way of maintaining focus and connecting with the Full Moon's energy. Are you ready to go? Let's begin!

What rules, conditions or beliefs stop you from truly loving yourself? How can you release these limitations so you can love yourself even more?

Finish this sentence (don't over think it, just answer it!): *I know when it's my intuition nudging me as opposed to my ego because my body physically gives me signs such as…*

*Practice using your intuition more and these signs will become clearer*

Date:

# FULL MOON
*Oracle Card Spread*

Record your Full Moon oracle spread here (if you feel called to do one) and consider how the messages that you receive can be applied to where you are in life right now and where you're going.

Date:

# FULL MOON
## Journaling Opportunity

"Confidence comes not from always being right but from not fearing to be wrong" - *Peter McIntyre*

### Self Love Reminder

Get your YES on: Did you know that many synchronistic opportunities that serve to move you closer to fulfilling your desires and goals get pushed aside because of the word, 'No'? Constantly saying No to life is like shutting the manifestation door and locking it with a deadlock. So, schedule a 'Yes' day (why not start now!). You'll be saying 'Yes' to opportunities that present themselves to you and confidently go where you would have otherwise said 'No'. (Note: You're allowed to say no if those opportunities overstep your boundaries.) This is your chance to witness just how synchronistic life can be.

Date:

# FULL MOON
## Shadow Work

Write a list or journal about all the things you're ready to let go of and why. You can also include those things that don't seem to relate to your overall plan. It's also a good idea to revisit the First Quarter section where you wrote about your fears and obstacles and consider if they're still relevant. The point is to just let it all out - don't hold back!

REMOVE THIS PAGE AND RIP IT UP OR BURN IT

MOONIFESTING

Date:

# FULL MOON
## Shadow Work

REMOVE THIS PAGE AND RIP IT UP OR BURN IT

*I lovingly accept and release these shadows*

Hand on heart, do you acknowledge your part in this; that it is your choice to either let go of these shadows or hold onto them? If you ticked 'Yes', then sign and date below as a way of declaring your intention to accept, let these shadows go, and move on with confidence.

**Yes** ☐    **No** ☐

_____    _____
Your Signature                                              Date

When you feel ready, burn or rip up this page as a symbol of release and liberation. Know that you are free of this energy that no longer serves your highest good.

Date:

# FULL MOON
## Journaling Opportunity

Now that you have released your shadows, you may like to sit in quiet contemplation and write or draw any thoughts, ideas, or impressions here.

What matters is how I handle an issue and work on how to respond to it differently – to catch myself while it's doing it's internal dance before it imparts my lips

MOONIFESTING

Date:

# WANING GIBBOUS

GRATITUDE | GIVE BACK | LOVE FULLY

This is your gratitude tealight ceremony where you can write down all the things you're grateful for on each tealight. If you're really feeling creative, why not colour each one in! You may even like to burn your own tealight and speak into the candle of all the things you love and appreciate.

*I am grateful for...*

Date:

# WANING GIBBOUS
## Journaling Opportunity

Use this space to journal what has been revealed to you so far during this lunar cycle. With those revelations, you may like to consider what you'll do about them now, what you have learned so far, and how you can apply that to your intentions. It's also a good time to reflect on whether your goals are for the good of others as well as for yourself. And if things aren't turning out as planned, try to use your intuition to sense if you need to accept a different outcome.

Date:

# WANING GIBBOUS
*Journaling Opportunity*

 *Give Back*

This is the perfect time to share your positive vibes with others. Refer to the Give Back page of this journal and do one or more of the suggested activities. Spread those high-vibes dear soul!

Date:

# THIRD QUARTER

RELEASE | LET GO | FORGIVENESS

Throughout the lunar cycle you may have been hurt, disappointed, broken or angered in different ways, so now is the time to let go of any pent up emotions and negative thoughts that cause suffering.

Reflect on this lunar cycle. Is there any negative energy you need to and want to let go of? What do you need (if anything) to bring balance to yourself? Journal about it here.

*Journal Prompt*

For those moments that didn't work out the way you wanted or expected, can you see an opportunity to learn from them? What did you learn?

Date:

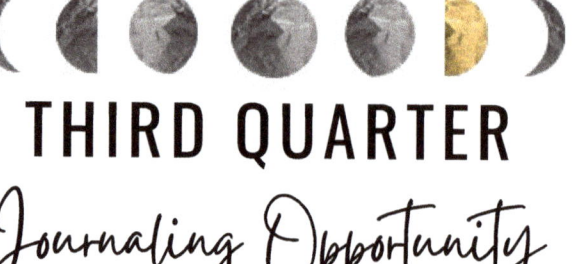

# THIRD QUARTER
## Journaling Opportunity

### Declutter Reminder
It's time to remove any distractions and excessive stress from your life. Refer to the Declutter portion of this book for ideas and inspiration on how to make space for the important things.

Date:

# THIRD QUARTER
## Prayer to the Universe

Sit somewhere comfortably where you won't be distracted. Take a few deep breaths to centre yourself. When you're ready read the following prayer to yourself slowly with the intention that this prayer is being directed to your soul and the Universe. You might like to do this a number of times as you allow the words to sink into your psyche. Try to *feel* into what the words represent for you. Lastly, say the prayer aloud as many times as you wish before finishing it off with another deep and cleansing breath.

**Note:** If you do not resonate with this prayer, then you may like to write your own for this particular Third Quarter Moon phase.

*I give away my self-doubt. My limiting beliefs. My fear of failure or success. My critical and judgemental voice. My pain of the past. My struggles. My anxieties. My despair. My shadows. My mistakes I cannot seem to forgive. I give away that which no longer serves me and hand it to you dear Universe. Please cleanse, clear, and transmute these and all attached memories across all time, space, dimensions, and realities. Thank you for filling my vessel with energy that empowers me to live my truth every day.*

*And so it is.*

Notes:

Date:

# WANING CRESCENT

SURRENDER | REFLECTION | REST & RESTORE

As you bring closure to this lunar cycle, now is the perfect time to honour and love your strengths, realisations and accomplishments.

Reflect on how far you have come. Journal all the ways you have grown and what you have learned over the past lunar cycle.

Talk to yourself. Replace critical self-talk with a more loving inner narrative. If you find this hard to do then imagine talking to yourself as a loving friend would. Give yourself the most inspiring pep talk imaginable – be kind, gentle and generous with the messages you send to yourself. Because what you say to yourself will either lift you up and inspire you or pull you down and force you to neglect your needs.

Date:

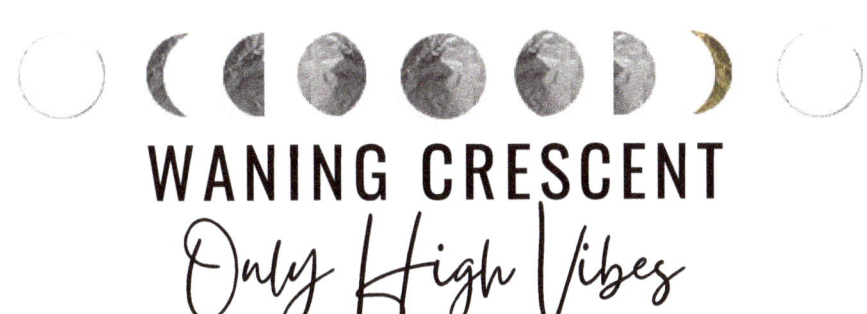

# WANING CRESCENT
## Only High Vibes

If you sense your mind, body, spirit is in need of a positive energy boost, write down what you could do to bring about those high vibes and then actively do them!

| Mind | Body | Spirit |
|------|------|--------|
| _____ | _____ | _____ |

In addition to that, take some time to let your mind, body, spirit rest as you get creative by colouring in this mandala.

MOONIFESTING

Lunar Cycle Dates:

HABIT TRACKER

HABIT | DATE

KEY:

# CYCLE PLAN

GOALS

DATE

MOOD TRACKER

Date:

# NEW MOON

New Beginnings | Unlimited Possibilities | Seeds of Intention

Are you ready explore a smorgasbord of unlimited possibilities? Now is the time to do it! Perhaps you're wanting to pick up from where you left off from the previous lunar cycle or maybe you're ready to set your focus and awareness on something entirely different. Either way, spend some quiet time and explore the Desire Question below whilst keeping in mind the results of your **Second Desires Road Map** (found in the Desires Road Map section of this journal) to create your ultimate wish list. Don't worry if the wish list is similar to the previous lunar cycle. The idea here is to just be in the moment, gather your intentions, and release them into the Universe.

## 'IF I COULD BE ANYTHING, DO ANYTHING, AND HAVE ANYTHING, WHAT WOULD IT BE?'

Remember; there's also the Be, Do and Have questions below that you can answer if you feel a bit stuck. These questions are a great way to get the creative juices flowing and open up the endless possibilities.

| BE | DO | HAVE |
|---|---|---|
| Who do I aspire to be and why? | What are 5 things I love to do that bring me joy? | What is my ideal health level? |
| What are the top 3 things I would like to be? (e.g. chef, florist, author etc) | If I had no commitments, how would I spend my days? | If money were no object, what tangible things would be in my life? |
| What are the most important things to me right now and why? | What are 3 big things I'd love to accomplish this year and why? | If I had $50,000 who would I give it to and why? |
| How do I want to feel right now? | When the final curtain closes, what would I regret not having done whilst I was still living? | What kind of world do I want to live in? |

Date:

# NEW MOON
My Ultimate Wish List / Desires

## 'IF I COULD BE ANYTHING, DO ANYTHING, AND HAVE ANYTHING, WHAT WOULD IT BE?'

Consider the Desire Question above whilst keeping in mind the results of your Second Desires Road Map. Now go ahead and make a list, journal, or draw all that you dream of. You can even stick inspirational cutouts from magazines and newspapers here too.

I now step out of my comfort zone to become the person I believe I can be

Date:

# NEW MOON
My Ultimate Wish List / Desires

'IF I COULD BE ANYTHING, DO ANYTHING, AND HAVE ANYTHING, WHAT WOULD IT BE?'

*And so it is*

Date:

# NEW MOON
## Oracle Card Spread

Record your New Moon oracle spread here (if you feel called to do one) and then consider how you could apply the messages you received to this lunar cycle and beyond.

Date:

# WAXING CRESCENT

Focus | Intention | Motivation | Curiosity

It's time to prioritise and refine your desires. Look at your wish list from the New Moon and categorise each desire into a realistic time period for when they may be achieved. Realise that the timeframe isn't set in stone but it can certainly help you decide on where your focus can be and what you intend to invest your energy on for the rest of the lunar cycle.

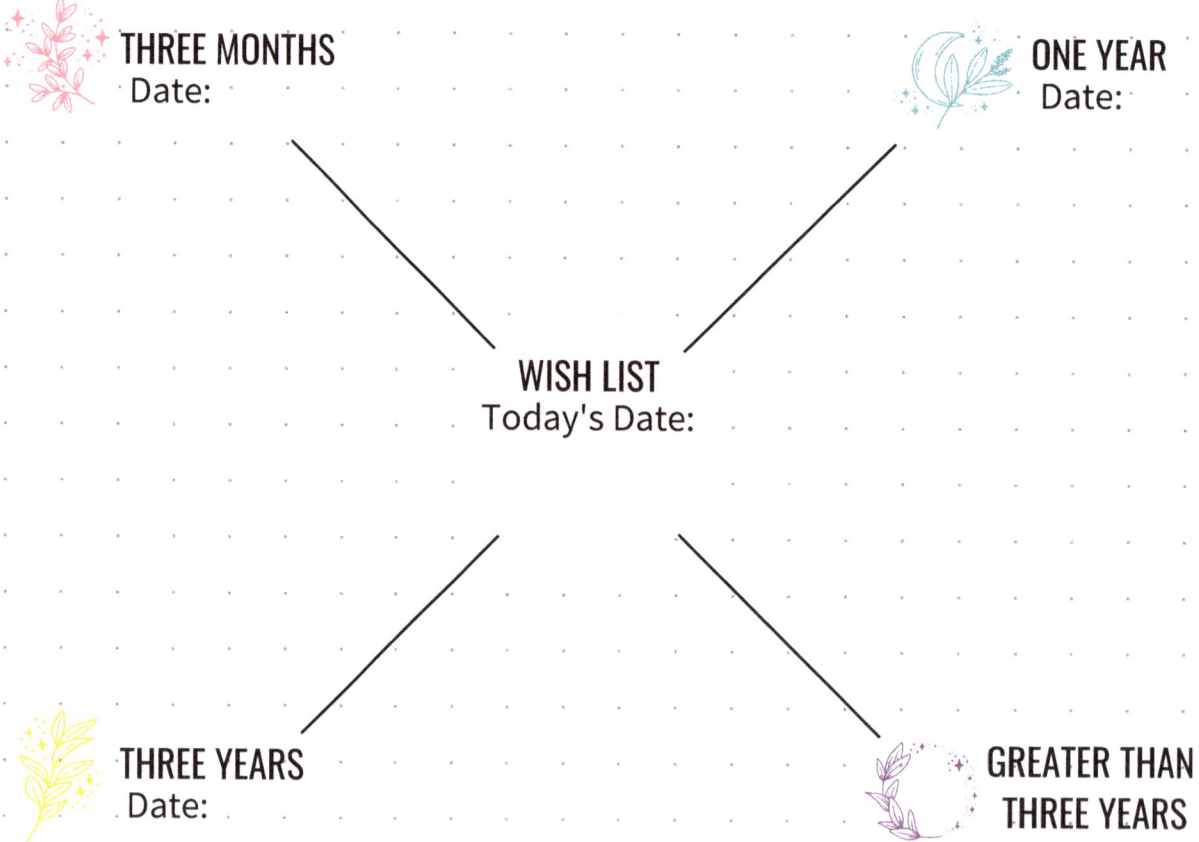

Now circle *one* desire from each timeframe (three months, one year, etc) that would have the most POSITIVE impact on YOUR LIFE and the LIVES OF OTHERS.

Date:

# WAXING CRESCENT

Focus | Intention | Motivation | Curiosity

From the desires you have circled on the previous page, answer the following questions:

*Which desire will bring me the **most positive impact** to my life and the lives of others RIGHT NOW?*

*How do I want to **feel** during this lunar cycle and which desire journey would create that same feeling?*

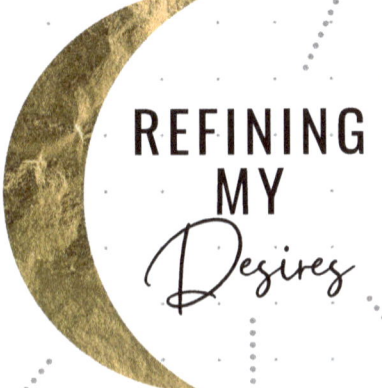

REFINING MY *Desires*

*My **heart** tells me I should choose the following desire to achieve...*

*My **mind** tells me I should choose the following desire to achieve...*

*Will I follow my **heart** or **mind** this time?*

MOONIFESTING

Date:

# WAXING CRESCENT

From your previous answers, which desire have you decided to focus on for the rest of this lunar cycle? If you have decided to work on more than one desire, make sure you're not overloading yourself with multiple tasks. Have confidence in your direction. You can achieve anything!

### The desire I have chosen
*to focus on during this lunar cycle is...*

*Because...*
*This your powerful motivator!*

*Affirmation*
Everyday I'm more aware of my thoughts and can easily tell when I'm lying to myself or in complete alignment with my divine nature

Date:

# WAXING CRESCENT

*This or something better...*

Journal or draw how you picture your desire to be when it manifests into your life. Write in present-tense as if it has already happened. Include as much detail as possible such as how you feel and what you see, hear, smell, and taste.

## TO DO...

Come back to this page every day to remind yourself of your intention or spend 5 minutes a day visualising in your mind's eye your desire coming to fruition (this is a powerful manifestation practice!).

### Inspiration

Nothing amazing and magical happened without stepping outside of your comfort zone. Stop playing it safe and make the decision to be all in – go for your dreams no matter how wild or crazy they may be.

MOONIFESTING

# MEDITATION MANTRA
## Happy, Well, and Safe

*Practice this meditation mantra if you're seeking love and kindness for yourself and for others*

**Note:** Before practicing this mantra, you may like to relook at the Meditation Mantra from the previous lunar cycle (titled Meditation Mantra - Divine Love) which includes detailed information on how to use mantras.

Sit in a comfortable position with one hand on your heart centre and the other on your abdomen. Feel your chest and abdomen rise and fall with each breath.

As you continue to breathe, say the words. **'May I be happy. May I be well. May I be safe. May I be peaceful and at ease'**.

After you have repeated this phrase for a few minutes picture a loved one in your mind's eye and repeat the phrase again only this time replace the 'I' with 'You'.

**May you be happy. May you be well. May you be safe. May you be peaceful and at ease.**

As you continue on with this meditation, you can start to direct this practice of loving-kindness out into the world. You can imagine sending the loving-kindness vibes to those who have hurt you or who you have difficult relationships with. And as you do so, you can bring greater peace to both yourself and others.

Date:

# FIRST QUARTER

Flexibility | Challenges | Decisions | Action

Use this space to write or draw all that you're afraid of or all the possible setbacks you believe could happen when it comes to fulfilling your chosen desire. Remember: If obstacles arise, you have the power to take bold steps for positive changes!

*Journal Prompt*

What does my fear hope to accomplish in my life? Do I want the same as what my fear wants?

MOONIFESTING

Date:

# FIRST QUARTER
## Journaling Opportunity

## Self Love Reminder
Try to steer clear of the 'Un' people – the people who are ungrateful, unkindly, unmotivated, unruly, unreasonable, untruthful, unnatural and above all, those who make you feel unloved and uncomfortable.

Date:

# FIRST QUARTER (AND BEYOND)
## *Desire Related Tasks*

Now is the perfect time to schedule out the smaller tasks which get you closer to your larger goal. Write down all the necessary tasks you sense are needed to achieve your desire.

**If your desire / goal is still the same from the previous lunar cycle** then reflect on whether additional tasks may need to be assigned and write them here.

EXAMPLE:
Create a vision board to reflect my desire

MY DESIRE / GOAL:

Realistic Due date:

## TO DO NEXT...
Number all the tasks in order so you end up with a sequential timeline

MOONIFESTING

Date:

# FIRST QUARTER (AND BEYOND)
*Action Plan*

Now select the **first 3 tasks** and write down, in sequential order, the detailed steps (e.g. what you need, how many, who to contact etc.) and resources needed to achieve each task. Next, add a realistic timeframe of when you expect to have each step completed taking into account other life responsibilities. **Then actively DO THEM!** Once a step has been achieved, tick it off and celebrate! Any changes that need to be made to the steps can be completed in the Changes column which you can do anytime throughout the Lunar cycle.

## INFO

| TASK | STEPS | RESOURCES | DUE | CHANGES | DONE |
|---|---|---|---|---|---|
| What is the task you need to complete to fulfill your desire? | What steps do you need to take to complete the task? | What resources will you need including material items, personal skills, and other people's involvement? | When can this step/s be realistically completed? | As you monitor your progress throughout the lunar cycle, are there any changes that may need to be made to the plan? | Tick each step once you have completed it and remember to CELEBRATE! |

Date:

# FIRST QUARTER (AND BEYOND)
*Action Plan*

| TASK | STEPS | RESOURCES | DUE | CHANGES | DONE |
|------|-------|-----------|-----|---------|------|
|      |       |           |     |         |      |

MOONIFESTING

Date:

# FIRST QUARTER (AND BEYOND)
*Action Plan*

| TASK | STEPS | RESOURCES | DUE | CHANGES | DONE |
|------|-------|-----------|-----|---------|------|
|      |       |           |     |         |      |
|      |       |           |     |         |      |
|      |       |           |     |         |      |
|      |       |           |     |         |      |
|      |       |           |     |         |      |

I AM
love
I AM
loving
I AM
lovable

Date:

# WAXING GIBBOUS

REFINEMENT | REFOCUS | CHANGES | PATIENCE

Use this space to journal how you're feeling about the progress of your plan and the journey you have travelled so far including any milestones (big or small) that you have achieved.

*Affirmation*

To experience the Universe and it's infinite love and power, I need to give it a chance

Date:

# WAXING GIBBOUS

*This or something better...*

As you reflect on your progress so far whilst checking in with your inner guidance, are there any changes that need to be made to your action plan?

**Note:** *If the changes still relate to your current plan,* be sure to update the Changes column of your Action Plan. Trust that your plan and support from the Universe will take you to the finish line.

*If the changes no longer relate to your current plan (which is completely okay!)* then write or draw your new plan below and complete the Refined Action Plan on the following page.

Date:

# WAXING GIBBOUS (AND BEYOND)
## Refined Action Plan

Write down **3 tasks** you could easily complete for the duration of this current lunar cycle and the associated steps needed to achieve each task. Remeber to tick off each one once they're done and celebrate your progress!

| TASK | STEPS | RESOURCES | DUE | DONE |
|------|-------|-----------|-----|------|
|      |       |           |     |      |
|      |       |           |     |      |
|      |       |           |     |      |

Date:

# WAXING GIBBOUS (AND BEYOND)
## Refined Action Plan

Write down **3 tasks** you could easily complete for the duration of this current lunar cycle and the associated steps needed to achieve each task.
Remeber to tick off each one once they're done and celebrate your progress!

| TASK | STEPS | RESOURCES | DUE | DONE |
|------|-------|-----------|-----|------|
|      |       |           |     |      |

Date:

# FULL MOON

RELEASE SETBACKS | CELEBRATE | SELF-LOVE

It's time to become aware of what needs to be seen and understood (Shadow Work) in order to release any setbacks. It's also a time to celebrate your beautiful nature and the magical life you're leading. As a gentle reminder (and if you haven't already) you may like to practice a specific Full Moon ritual (see The Moon Ritual section, particularly the Quick Moon Ritual Guide Step-by-Step section in this book which gives you all the information on how to do one) as a way of maintaining focus and connecting with the Full Moon's energy. Are you ready to go? Let's begin!

What do you need to be more at peace with yourself? How can you get there?

Finish this sentence (don't over think it, just answer it!): *I know I'm doing something that matters to me when I feel...*

*Invite more of this feeling into your life!*

Date:

# FULL MOON
*Oracle Card Spread*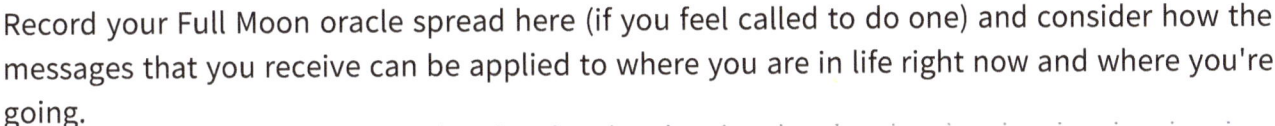

Record your Full Moon oracle spread here (if you feel called to do one) and consider how the messages that you receive can be applied to where you are in life right now and where you're going.

MOONIFESTING

Date:

# FULL MOON
## Journaling Opportunity

"There are only two days in the year that nothing can be done. One is called Yesterday and the other is called Tomorrow. Today is the right day to Love, Believe, Do and mostly Live" - *Dalai Lama XIV*

## Self Love Reminder

Set up a bliss station: Reflect on where you spend most of your time and place some of your favourite things there such as inspiring artwork, essential oils, plants, a photo of your favourite place to visit; anything that brings you a smile. Because when you smile, you create those feel-good vibes. If you've already got a bliss station, relook at it and see if anything needs to be removed or swapped for something else. Everything must bring you joy!

Date:

# FULL MOON
## Shadow Work

Write a list or journal about all the things you're ready to let go of and why. You can also include those things that don't seem to relate to your overall plan. It's also a good idea to revisit the First Quarter section where you wrote about your fears and obstacles and consider if they're still relevant. The point is to just let it all out - don't hold back!

REMOVE THIS PAGE AND RIP IT UP OR BURN IT

Date:

# FULL MOON
## Shadow Work

REMOVE THIS PAGE AND RIP IT UP OR BURN IT

*I lovingly accept and release these shadows*

Hand on heart, do you acknowledge your part in this; that it is your choice to either let go of these shadows or hold onto them? If you ticked 'Yes', then sign and date below as a way of declaring your intention to accept, let these shadows go, and move on with confidence.

**Yes** ☐   **No** ☐

_____   _____
Your Signature                                    Date

When you feel ready, burn or rip up this page as a symbol of release and liberation. Know that you are free of this energy that no longer serves your highest good.

Date:

# FULL MOON
## Journaling Opportunity

Now that you have released your shadows, you may like to sit in quiet contemplation and write or draw any thoughts, ideas, or impressions here.

Change always begins with me – I can, I will, I am

Date:

# WANING GIBBOUS

GRATITUDE | GIVE BACK | LOVE FULLY

This is your gratitude jar where you can write in it all the things you're grateful for; people, places, experiences, feelings, realisations..anything! You may even like to keep a real gratitude jar near your sacred space and place gratitude notes in it everyday.

*I am grateful for....*

Date:

# WANING GIBBOUS
## Journaling Opportunity

Use this space to journal what has been revealed to you so far during this lunar cycle. With those revelations, you may like to consider what you'll do about them now, what you have learned so far, and how you can apply that to your intentions. It's also a good time to reflect on whether your goals are for the good of others as well as for yourself. And if things aren't turning out as planned, try to use your intuition to sense if you need to accept a different outcome.

Date:

# WANING GIBBOUS
## Journaling Opportunity

This is the perfect time to share your positive vibes with others. Refer to the Give Back page of this journal and do one or more of the suggested activities. Spread those high-vibes dear soul!

Date:

# THIRD QUARTER

RELEASE | LET GO | FORGIVENESS

Throughout the lunar cycle you may have been hurt, disappointed, broken or angered in different ways, so now is the time to let go of any pent up emotions and negative thoughts that cause suffering.

Reflect on this lunar cycle. Is there any negative energy you need to and want to let go of? What do you need (if anything) to bring balance to yourself? Journal about it here.

## Journal Prompt

On a scale from 1 to 10, where 1 is someone who goes with the flow and 10 is a control freak, where would you place yourself and why? What insights or negative judgements rise within you about the number you've chosen on the scale? Journal it here.

MOONIFESTING

Date:

# THIRD QUARTER
## Journaling Opportunity

It's time to remove any distractions and excessive stress from your life. Refer to the Declutter portion of this book for ideas and inspiration on how to make space for the important things.

Date:

# THIRD QUARTER
## *Prayer to the Universe*

Sit somewhere comfortably where you won't be distracted. Take a few deep breaths to centre yourself. When you're ready read the following prayer to yourself slowly with the intention that this prayer is being directed to your soul and the Universe. You might like to do this a number of times as you allow the words to sink into your psyche. Try to *feel* into what the words represent for you. Lastly, say the prayer aloud as many times as you wish before finishing it off with another deep and cleansing breath.

**Note:** If you do not resonate with this prayer, then you may like to write your own for this particular Third Quarter Moon phase.

*One day at a time, I'm unlearning and remembering. I'm unlearning the false perceptions of the world that I chose to believe in, and the rules that told me on how I should live my life and who I should be. I'm unlearning the stories of I'm not good enough, if I'm not struggling or suffering then I won't achieve my goals, or that I must do extraordinary things to receive love. The stories go on but each day I commit to unlearning and remembering.*
*To go deeper and bigger.*

*And so it is.*

Notes:

Date:

# WANING CRESCENT

SURRENDER | REFLECTION | REST & RESTORE

As you bring closure to this lunar cycle, now is the perfect time to honour and love your strengths, realisations and accomplishments.

Reflect on how far you have come. Journal all the ways you have grown and what you have learned over the past lunar cycle.

Breathe it Out. Sit or lay down in a quiet and safe place such as on your bed or the floor and put one of your hands on your abdomen. Breathe in for a slow count of three, and then breathe out for the same slow count of three. Feel your abdomen rise and fall as you breathe in and out. Repeat five times or as long as you need to feel relaxed.

Date:

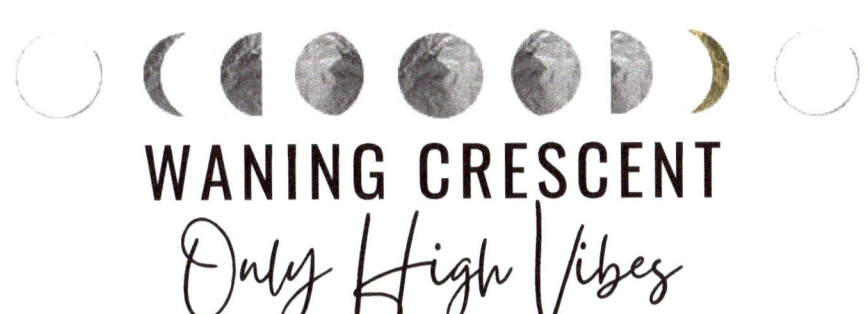

# WANING CRESCENT
*Only High Vibes*

If you sense your mind, body, spirit is in need of a positive energy boost, write down what you could do to bring about those high vibes and then actively do them!

_____    _____    _____
*Mind*                          *Body*                             *Spirit*

In addition to that, take some time to let your mind, body, spirit rest as you get creative by colouring in this mandala.

MOONIFESTING

# THE Lunar

Lunar Cycle Dates:

HABIT TRACKER

| HABIT | DATE |
|---|---|

KEY:

# CYCLE PLAN

GOALS

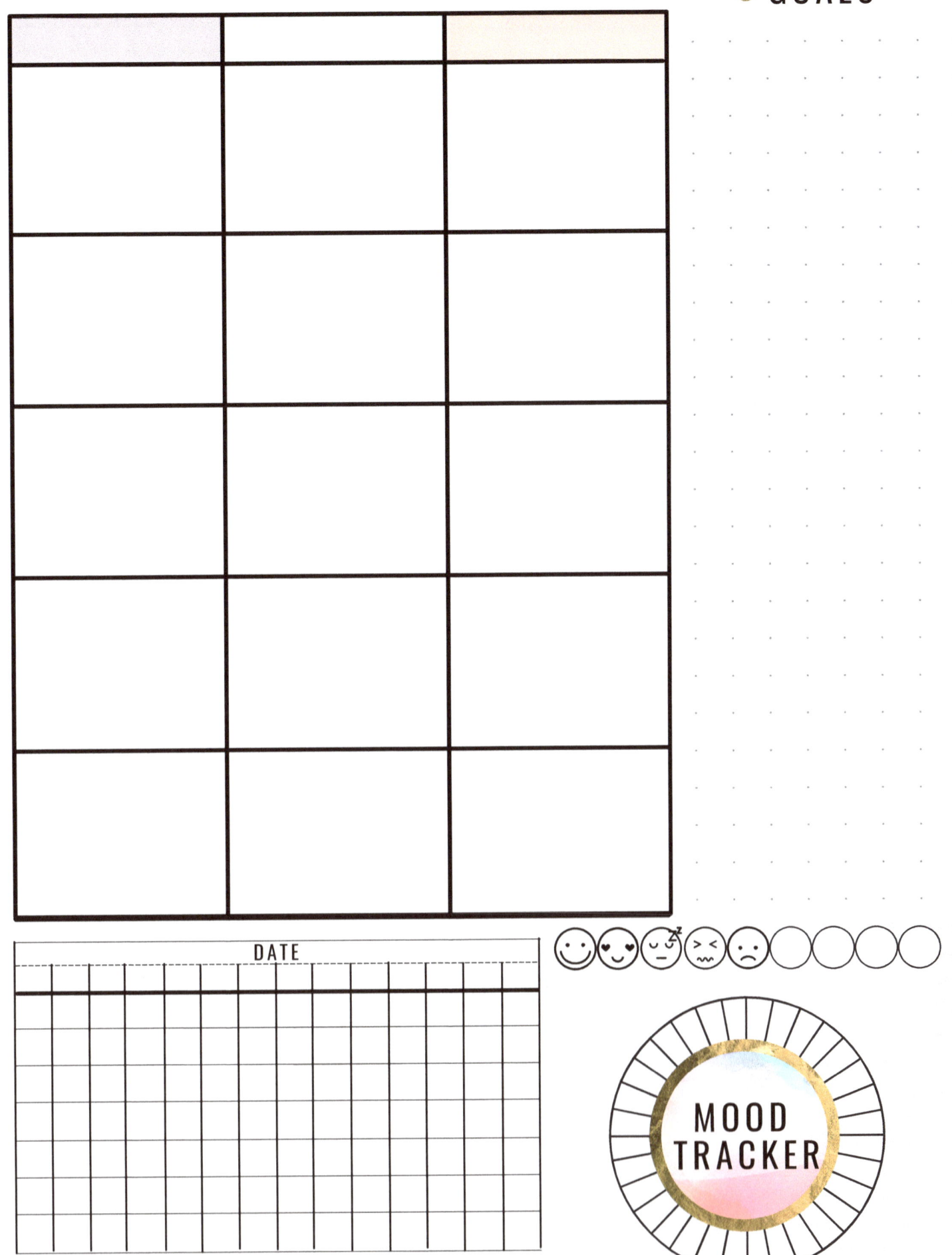

DATE

MOOD TRACKER

Date:

# NEW MOON

New Beginnings | Unlimited Possibilities | Seeds of Intention

It's new beginnings time! Let's create some magic! Firstly, go to the **Third Desires Road Map** (found in the Desires Road Map section of this journal) and complete it to see just how balanced and harmonious your life is right now. This will help you gauge where your soul wants to be and what your intentions are for this New Moon. Then once you have done that, come back here and continue working with the New Moon's energy.

### 'IF I COULD BE ANYTHING, DO ANYTHING, AND HAVE ANYTHING, WHAT WOULD IT BE?'

To create new intentions for this lunar cycle, keep in mind the results of the Third Desires Road Map and the Desire Question above. You may even want to answer the Be, Do and Have questions below if you feel a bit stuck - the ways to truly know and understand what your soul wants in life is limitless and so too are the possibilities of how your life can be!

| BE | DO | HAVE |
|---|---|---|
| Who do I aspire to be and why? | What are 5 things I love to do that bring me joy? | What is my ideal health level? |
| What are the top 3 things I would like to be? (e.g. chef, florist, author etc) | If I had no commitments, how would I spend my days? | If money were no object, what tangible things would be in my life? |
| What are the most important things to me right now and why? | What are 3 big things I'd love to accomplish this year and why? | If I had $50,000 who would I give it to and why? |
| How do I want to feel right now? | When the final curtain closes, what would I regret not having done whilst I was still living? | What kind of world do I want to live in? |

Date:

# NEW MOON
My Ultimate Wish List / Desires

## 'IF I COULD BE ANYTHING, DO ANYTHING, AND HAVE ANYTHING, WHAT WOULD IT BE?'

Consider the Desire Question above whilst keeping in mind the results of your Third Desires Road Map. Now go ahead and make a list, journal, or draw all that you dream of. You can even stick inspirational cutouts from magazines and newspapers here too.

I intend to live this day to the fullest – nothing can pull me down now

MOONIFESTING

Date:

# NEW MOON
My Ultimate Wish List / Desires

**'IF I COULD BE ANYTHING, DO ANYTHING, AND HAVE ANYTHING, WHAT WOULD IT BE?'**

*And so it is*

Date:

# NEW MOON
*Oracle Card Spread*

Record your New Moon oracle spread here (if you feel called to do one) and then consider how you could apply the messages you received to this lunar cycle and beyond.

MOONIFESTING

Date:

# WAXING CRESCENT

Focus | Intention | Motivation | Curiosity

It's time to prioritise and refine your desires. Look at your wish list from the New Moon and categorise each desire into a realistic time period for when they may be achieved. Realise that the timeframe isn't set in stone but it can certainly help you decide on where your focus can be and what you intend to invest your energy on for the rest of the lunar cycle.

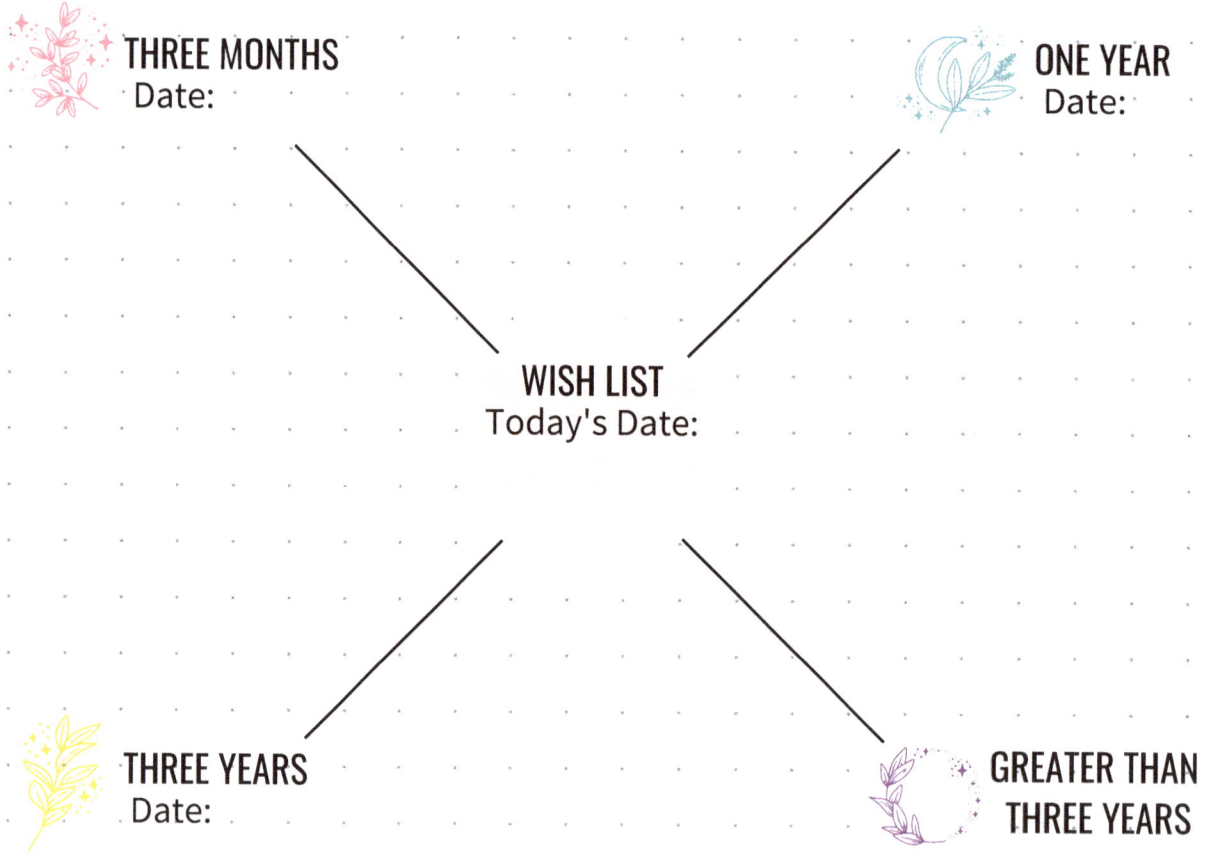

Now circle *one* desire from each timeframe (three months, one year, etc) that would have the most POSITIVE impact on YOUR LIFE and the LIVES OF OTHERS.

Date:

# WAXING CRESCENT

Focus | Intention | Motivation | Curiosity

From the desires you have circled on the previous page, answer the following questions:

*Which desire will bring me the **most positive impact** to my life and the lives of others RIGHT NOW?*

*How do I want to **feel** during this lunar cycle and which desire journey would create that same feeling?*

### REFINING MY *Desires*

*My **heart** tells me I should choose the following desire to achieve...*

*My **mind** tells me I should choose the following desire to achieve...*

*Will I follow my **heart** or **mind** this time?*

MOONIFESTING

Date:

# WAXING CRESCENT

From your previous answers, which desire have you decided to focus on for the rest of this lunar cycle? If you have decided to work on more than one desire, make sure you're not overloading yourself with multiple tasks. Have confidence in your direction. You can achieve anything!

### The desire I have chosen
*to focus on during this lunar cycle is...*

*Because...*
This your powerful motivator!

*Affirmation*

More and more happiness is filling my whole being – I can feel it and I know it

Date:

# WAXING CRESCENT

*This or something better...*

Journal or draw how you picture your desire to be when it manifests into your life. Write in present-tense as if it has already happened. Include as much detail as possible such as how you feel and what you see, hear, smell, and taste.

## TO DO...

Come back to this page every day to remind yourself of your intention or spend 5 minutes a day visualising in your mind's eye your desire coming to fruition (this is a powerful manifestation practice!).

*Inspiration*

If you're completely certain of the outcome of your desires, then you can afford to relax. Do what you feel spiritually inspired to do and nothing more. Relax. Chill. It's all good.

# MEDITATION FOR
## *Self Love*

*Practice this self love meditation any time you're experiencing frustration, doubt or judgement toward yourself, or even when you're in need of some high-vibe love regardless of what's going on today*

Begin with a slow and long deep breath. On the inhale, feel your breath filling your body and, on the exhale, feel the breath releasing and letting go of all stress, worry, or tension. Take another breath in, feel your body relax and let go even more, deeper down now. Exhaling away any stress or thoughts that take you away from this moment. On the next breath in, breathe in the energy of love – see it as a beautiful white or golden light. See this light moving with your breath and illuminating every cell of your body. And just notice your body relaxing even more as your body continues to fill up with this beautiful light. As you exhale, witness the release any thoughts or beliefs that may make you feel doubt or unworthy of this light. Let it go now as you exhale. Remembering that you're in charge. You can choose what stays and what goes. Allow your body to continue to fill up with this magnificent light and notice each cell embody and beam with this golden light – glowing with vitality.

As you look closely, each cell is smiling back at you as it's filled with joy. This makes you smile. So, allow yourself to smile. Feel the joy that is coming up through your being. Feel the expansiveness – this energy in your body. You are worthy and deserving of this love. You don't have to do anything to receive it. All that's required is that you're open to receiving it as it's always there for you. It's yours– any other belief is an illusion from the mind because you are love and only love. So, continue to breath in and out. Savour in this light. Notice how it extends now beyond your physical body and allow it to continue to expand as much as it wants. Feel it as you watch it expand more and more outside your body. Breathing in and breathing out. This light is who you really are. Only love, nothing else. Let it in. Let it in.

Date:

# FIRST QUARTER

Flexibility | Challenges | Decisions | Action

Use this space to write or draw all that you're afraid of or all the possible setbacks you believe could happen when it comes to fulfilling your chosen desire. Remember: If obstacles arise, you have the power to take bold steps for positive changes!

*Journal Prompt*

If I had a conversation with my future self who has already achieved their wildest dreams, what is their advice or message for me about how they did it?

Date:

# FIRST QUARTER
## Journaling Opportunity

### Self Love Reminder

Get comfortable with the idea that it's okay to ask for help – there's nothing shameful or weak about it. Choose a 48-hour period to mindfully notice how often people reach out for help, or how often you're helpful to others, so you can become aware of the natural and organic exchange of people helping each other daily. Being open to receive help from others and the Universe allows you to receive all that you deserve.

Date:

# FIRST QUARTER (AND BEYOND)
## Desire Related Tasks

Now is the perfect time to schedule out the smaller tasks which get you closer to your larger goal. Write down all the necessary tasks you sense are needed to achieve your desire.

**If your desire / goal is still the same from the previous lunar cycle** then reflect on whether additional tasks may need to be assigned and write them here.

EXAMPLE:
Create a vision board to reflect my desire

MY DESIRE / GOAL:

Realistic Due date:

## TO DO NEXT...
Number all the tasks in order so you end up with a sequential timeline

Date:

# FIRST QUARTER (AND BEYOND)
## Action Plan

Now select the **first 3 tasks** and write down, in sequential order, the detailed steps (e.g. what you need, how many, who to contact etc.) and resources needed to achieve each task. Next, add a realistic timeframe of when you expect to have each step completed taking into account other life responsibilities. **Then actively DO THEM!** Once a step has been achieved, tick it off and celebrate! Any changes that need to be made to the steps can be completed in the Changes column which you can do anytime throughout the Lunar cycle.

## INFO

| TASK | STEPS | RESOURCES | DUE | CHANGES | DONE |
|---|---|---|---|---|---|
| What is the task you need to complete to fulfill your desire? | What steps do you need to take to complete the task? | What resources will you need including material items, personal skills, and other people's involvement? | When can this step/s be realistically completed? | As you monitor your progress throughout the lunar cycle, are there any changes that may need to be made to the plan? | Tick each step once you have completed it and remember to CELEBRATE! |

Date:

# FIRST QUARTER (AND BEYOND)
*Action Plan*

| TASK | STEPS | RESOURCES | DUE | CHANGES | DONE |
|------|-------|-----------|-----|---------|------|
|      |       |           |     |         |      |

Date:

# FIRST QUARTER (AND BEYOND)
*Action Plan*

| TASK | STEPS | RESOURCES | DUE | CHANGES | DONE |
|------|-------|-----------|-----|---------|------|
|      |       |           |     |         |      |
|      |       |           |     |         |      |
|      |       |           |     |         |      |
|      |       |           |     |         |      |
|      |       |           |     |         |      |

CONNECTION WITH MY **INNER SPIRIT** BRINGS ME CONSTANT *peace & joy*

Date:

# WAXING GIBBOUS

REFINEMENT | REFOCUS | CHANGES | PATIENCE

Use this space to journal how you're feeling about the progress of your plan and the journey you have travelled so far including any milestones (big or small) that you have achieved.

*Affirmation*

With every breath I take, I embody love, light, truth and peace

Date:

# WAXING GIBBOUS
*This or something better...*

As you reflect on your progress so far whilst checking in with your inner guidance, are there any changes that need to be made to your action plan?

**Note:** *If the changes still relate to your current plan*, be sure to update the Changes column of your Action Plan. Trust that your plan and support from the Universe will take you to the finish line.

*If the changes no longer relate to your current plan (which is completely okay!)* then write or draw your new plan below and complete the Refined Action Plan on the following page.

Date:

# WAXING GIBBOUS (AND BEYOND)
## Refined Action Plan

Write down **3 tasks** you could easily complete for the duration of this current lunar cycle and the associated steps needed to achieve each task. Remeber to tick off each one once they're done and celebrate your progress!

| TASK | STEPS | RESOURCES | DUE | DONE |
|------|-------|-----------|-----|------|
|      |       |           |     |      |
|      |       |           |     |      |
|      |       |           |     |      |

Date:

# WAXING GIBBOUS (AND BEYOND)
## Refined Action Plan

Write down **3 tasks** you could easily complete for the duration of this current lunar cycle and the associated steps needed to achieve each task. Remember to tick off each one once they're done and celebrate your progress!

| TASK | STEPS | RESOURCES | DUE | DONE |
|------|-------|-----------|-----|------|
|      |       |           |     |      |

Date:

# FULL MOON

RELEASE SETBACKS | CELEBRATE | SELF-LOVE

It's time to become aware of what needs to be seen and understood (Shadow Work) in order to release any setbacks. It's also a time to celebrate your beautiful nature and the magical life you're leading. As a gentle reminder (and if you haven't already) you may like to practice a specific Full Moon ritual (see The Moon Ritual section, particularly the Quick Moon Ritual Guide Step-by-Step section in this book which gives you all the information on how to do one) as a way of maintaining focus and connecting with the Full Moon's energy. Are you ready to go? Let's begin!

List at least 10 things you love and value about yourself.

Finish this sentence (don't over think it, just answer it!): *I can be more of a best friend to myself by...*

*Invite more of this feeling into your life!*

Date:

# FULL MOON
## Oracle Card Spread

Record your Full Moon oracle spread here (if you feel called to do one) and consider how the messages that you receive can be applied to where you are in life right now and where you're going.

Date:

# FULL MOON
## Journaling Opportunity

"The move that you're afraid to make could be the one that changes everything" - *Unknown*

### Self Love Reminder

Love thy body: Your body is the vessel that provides you this opportunity of life on Earth, so yes, it's pretty darn important. So as you go about loving yourself, it's essential that part of those high vibes are extended to your body. How you feel about your body affects how you feel about yourself. So make a body agreement with yourself and choose something you can do on a regular basis that will show your body just how much you love it – move it, nourish it, and let it unwind.

Date:

# FULL MOON
## Shadow Work

Write a list or journal about all the things you're ready to let go of and why. You can also include those things that don't seem to relate to your overall plan. It's also a good idea to revisit the First Quarter section where you wrote about your fears and obstacles and consider if they're still relevant. The point is to just let it all out - don't hold back!

REMOVE THIS PAGE AND RIP IT UP OR BURN IT

Date:

# FULL MOON
## Shadow Work

REMOVE THIS PAGE AND RIP IT UP OR BURN IT

*I lovingly accept and release these shadows*

Hand on heart, do you acknowledge your part in this; that it is your choice to either let go of these shadows or hold onto them? If you ticked 'Yes', then sign and date below as a way of declaring your intention to accept, let these shadows go, and move on with confidence.

**Yes** ☐     **No** ☐

_____       _____
Your Signature     Date

When you feel ready, burn or rip up this page as a symbol of release and liberation. Know that you are free of this energy that no longer serves your highest good.

Date:

# FULL MOON
*Journaling Opportunity*

Now that you have released your shadows, you may like to sit in quiet contemplation and write or draw any thoughts, ideas, or impressions here.

I am living my manifested outcome that I dreamed into existence

MOONIFESTING

Date:

# WANING GIBBOUS

GRATITUDE | GIVE BACK | LOVE FULLY

Imagine you're standing in a crystal cave. In this sacred space, write down on each of these crystals below all the things you're grateful for particularly the things that make you feel energised, calm and at peace. If you're really feeling creative, why not colour each one in!

*I am grateful for...*

Date:

# WANING GIBBOUS
## Journaling Opportunity

Use this space to journal what has been revealed to you so far during this lunar cycle. With those revelations, you may like to consider what you'll do about them now, what you have learned so far, and how you can apply that to your intentions. It's also a good time to reflect on whether your goals are for the good of others as well as for yourself. And if things aren't turning out as planned, try to use your intuition to sense if you need to accept a different outcome.

MOONIFESTING

Date:

# WANING GIBBOUS
*Journaling Opportunity*

## Give Back

This is the perfect time to share your positive vibes with others. Refer to the Give Back page of this journal and do one or more of the suggested activities. Spread those high-vibes dear soul!

Date:

# THIRD QUARTER

RELEASE | LET GO | FORGIVENESS

Throughout the lunar cycle you may have been hurt, disappointed, broken or angered in different ways, so now is the time to let go of any pent up emotions and negative thoughts that cause suffering.

Reflect on this lunar cycle. Is there any negative energy you need to and want to let go of? What do you need (if anything) to bring balance to yourself? Journal about it here.

*Journal Prompt*

Be honest – were you your own best friend throughout this lunar cycle? What could you do differently?

Date:

# THIRD QUARTER
## Journaling Opportunity

### Declutter Reminder

It's time to remove any distractions and excessive stress from your life. Refer to the Declutter portion of this book for ideas and inspiration on how to make space for the important things.

Date:

# THIRD QUARTER
## *Prayer to the Universe*

Sit somewhere comfortably where you won't be distracted. Take a few deep breaths to centre yourself. When you're ready read the following prayer to yourself slowly with the intention that this prayer is being directed to your soul and the Universe. You might like to do this a number of times as you allow the words to sink into your psyche. Try to *feel* into what the words represent for you. Lastly, say the prayer aloud as many times as you wish before finishing it off with another deep and cleansing breath.

**Note:** If you do not resonate with this prayer, then you may like to write your own for this particular Third Quarter Moon phase.

*All is well. I trust and know that everything happening within and around me is being taken care of by the spirit and source of love within me. I am open to creative solutions as I release my limiting beliefs and tune into the spark and source of love that is me. I welcome the presence of higher beings and the light of the world as the energy that guides, protects, loves, and supports me. I am safe. It's okay to feel good now. I welcome a good-feeling vibration and I choose to feel good right now. I know that all is well.*

*And so it is.*

Notes:

Date:

# WANING CRESCENT

SURRENDER | REFLECTION | REST & RESTORE

As you bring closure to this lunar cycle, now is the perfect time to honour and love your strengths, realisations and accomplishments.

Reflect on how far you have come. Journal all the ways you have grown and what you have learned over the past lunar cycle.

Be a 99 year old. One of my Grandmother's favourite quotes is 'this too shall pass' – words to describe that even if you're experiencing something wonderful or something unpleasant; nothing lasts forever. So, in times of distress, breathe deeply, appreciate the lesson that is being offered to you, and trust that you can carry on even during challenging times. Likewise, when things are going well. Breathe in gratitude for the experience and allow your spirit to become a sponge – soaking it all in and cherishing the now.

Date:

# WANING CRESCENT
## Only High Vibes

If you sense your mind, body, spirit is in need of a positive energy boost, write down what you could do to bring about those high vibes and then actively do them!

_____  _____  _____
*Mind*          *Body*          *Spirit*

In addition to that, take some time to let your mind, body, spirit rest as you get creative by colouring in this mandala.

MOONIFESTING

Lunar Cycle Dates:

## HABIT TRACKER

HABIT | DATE

KEY:

# CYCLE PLAN

● GOALS

DATE

MOOD TRACKER

Date:

# NEW MOON

New Beginnings | Unlimited Possibilities | Seeds of Intention

It's another beautiful time to start something new or pick up from where you left off from the previous lunar cycle! Use this time to explore the Desire Question below whilst keeping in mind the results of your **Third Desires Road Map** (found in the Desires Road Map section of this journal) to create your ultimate wish list. Don't worry if the wish list is similar to the previous lunar cycle. The idea here is to just be in the moment, gather your intentions, and release them into the Universe.

## 'IF I COULD BE ANYTHING, DO ANYTHING, AND HAVE ANYTHING, WHAT WOULD IT BE?'

And remember, if you're still a little stuck and just don't know where to start, you can also explore and answer the Be, Do and Have questions below to open yourself up to inspiration.

| BE | DO | HAVE |
|---|---|---|
| Who do I aspire to be and why? | What are 5 things I love to do that bring me joy? | What is my ideal health level? |
| What are the top 3 things I would like to be? (e.g. chef, florist, author etc) | If I had no commitments, how would I spend my days? | If money were no object, what tangible things would be in my life? |
| What are the most important things to me right now and why? | What are 3 big things I'd love to accomplish this year and why? | If I had $50,000 who would I give it to and why? |
| How do I want to feel right now? | When the final curtain closes, what would I regret not having done whilst I was still living? | What kind of world do I want to live in? |

Date:

# NEW MOON
My Ultimate Wish List / Desires

## 'IF I COULD BE ANYTHING, DO ANYTHING, AND HAVE ANYTHING, WHAT WOULD IT BE?'

Consider the Desire Question above whilst keeping in mind the results of your Third Desires Road Map. Now go ahead and make a list, journal, or draw all that you dream of. You can even stick inspirational cutouts from magazines and newspapers here too.

New and exciting opportunities are ahead of me – I am creating my own destiny

Date:

# NEW MOON
My Ultimate Wish List / Desires

**'IF I COULD BE ANYTHING, DO ANYTHING, AND HAVE ANYTHING, WHAT WOULD IT BE?'**

*And so it is*

Date:

# NEW MOON
## Oracle Card Spread

Record your New Moon oracle spread here (if you feel called to do one) and then consider how you could apply the messages you received to this lunar cycle and beyond.

Date:

# WAXING CRESCENT

Focus | Intention | Motivation | Curiosity

It's time to prioritise and refine your desires. Look at your wish list from the New Moon and categorise each desire into a realistic time period for when they may be achieved. Realise that the timeframe isn't set in stone but it can certainly help you decide on where your focus can be and what you intend to invest your energy on for the rest of the lunar cycle.

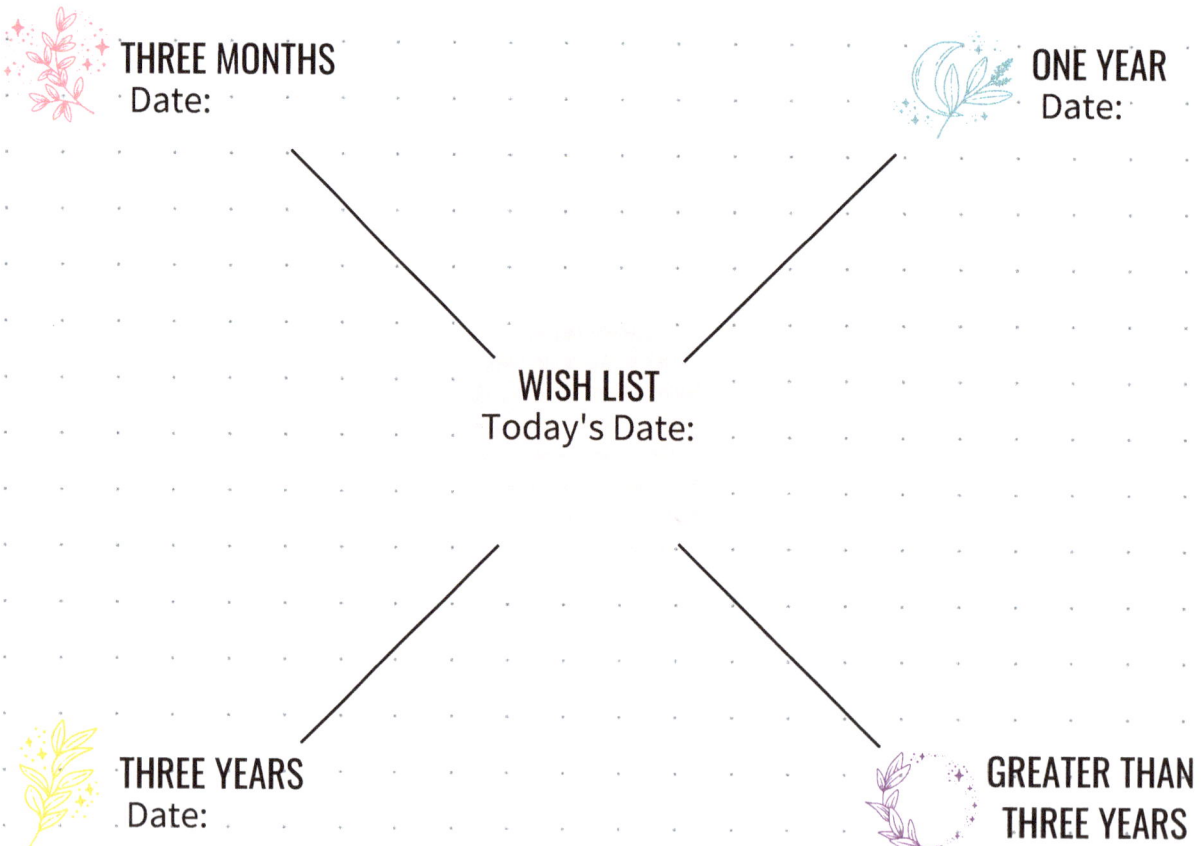

Now circle *one* desire from each timeframe (three months, one year, etc) that would have the most POSITIVE impact on YOUR LIFE and the LIVES OF OTHERS.

Date:

# WAXING CRESCENT

Focus | Intention | Motivation | Curiosity

From the desires you have circled on the previous page, answer the following questions:

*Which desire will bring me the **most positive impact** to my life and the lives of others RIGHT NOW?*

*How do I want to **feel** during this lunar cycle and which desire journey would create that same feeling?*

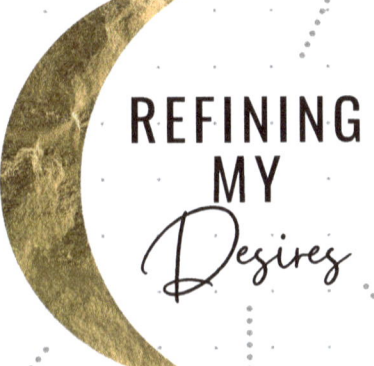

REFINING MY *Desires*

*My **heart** tells me I should choose the following desire to achieve...*

*My **mind** tells me I should choose the following desire to achieve...*

*Will I follow my **heart** or **mind** this time?*

MOONIFESTING

Date:

# WAXING CRESCENT

From your previous answers, which desire have you decided to focus on for the rest of this lunar cycle? If you have decided to work on more than one desire, make sure you're not overloading yourself with multiple tasks. Have confidence in your direction. You can achieve anything!

## The desire I have chosen
*to focus on during this lunar cycle is...*

### Because...
*This your powerful motivator!*

### Affirmation

I am willing to believe that I'm a powerful co-creator of my life experience – I can make the rules and decide who I want to be

Date:

# WAXING CRESCENT

*This or something better...*

Journal or draw how you picture your desire to be when it manifests into your life. Write in present-tense as if it has already happened. Include as much detail as possible such as how you feel and what you see, hear, smell, and taste.

## TO DO...
Come back to this page every day to remind yourself of your intention or spend 5 minutes a day visualising in your mind's eye your desire coming to fruition (this is a powerful manifestation practice!).

### Inspiration
Trust the process. You might have an idea of how your dreams and desires will unfold but the Universe may just have a much greater and better plan for you. Accept your greatness now and trust that the Universe will soon catch up to your glorious energy.

MOONIFESTING

# MEDITATION FOR
## *Clearing Negative Energy from the Body*

*This cleansing meditation will have you connect with your guides to help you clear away any stagnant and negative energy that you no longer want or need. If you've been feeling lethargic, stressed and life has been chaotic, then this meditation can help!*

Find a comfortable position and place your palms facing up to allow yourself to receive and let go. Close your eyes and roll them up toward your third eye. Inhale and feel your diaphragm extend, and as you exhale, feel it contract. Just keep this natural rhythm of breathing – deeply inhaling and extending, exhaling and contracting. As you stay in this relaxed state, call upon the guidance of your highest truth and compassion to enter your space – the energy of your own wisdom and from the teachers that came before you. And simply hold this energy within the room that you're in. Feel this energy surrounding you like a warm and comforting blanket. And just know that this energy consists of divine entities who hold unconditional love for you, who protect you and who are helping you to wake up and remember who you are; the infinite, limitless and peaceful being.

And as you continue to breathe rhythmically, holding space for these divine beings of love and light, you can ask that they clear your space or vacuum all that you have been holding onto – all that no longer serves you; residual energy that is stagnant and obsolete. And just imagine these beautiful beings getting to work - clearing or vacuuming this stagnant energy from your spiritual, emotional and physical body starting from your toes and working their way up toward your knees, hips, abdomen, chest, arms, shoulders, throat, and all the way to the crown of your head…vacuuming and suctioning the out-dated energy. Lifting the tension, fear, struggles, and resistance to love. And as you continue to breathe deeply and witness the divine beings rebalancing your body, you can ask them to recycle, transform and transmute the negative energy so that as it re-enters your body, it is cleaned and cleared and vibrating at a frequency that is in harmony with your highest truth.

And when you feel it's time, take another deep breath in and simply watch the divine beings leave your space. Thank them for holding and clearing you and know that you can ask them to repeat this same practice anytime you feel you need it.

Date:

# FIRST QUARTER

Flexibility | Challenges | Decisions | Action

Use this space to write or draw all that you're afraid of or all the possible setbacks you believe could happen when it comes to fulfilling your chosen desire. Remember: If obstacles arise, you have the power to take bold steps for positive changes!

*Journal Prompt*

Am I comfortable around the thought of succeeding? Does it make me feel uneasy or embarrassed in any way? Why?

Date:

# FIRST QUARTER
## Journaling Opportunity

### Self Love Reminder

Either you control your thoughts or you allow outside forces to control them for you. But be warned that the outside forces often know nothing about your greatest potential, purpose, or just how deserving you are of a magical and joyous life.

Date:

# FIRST QUARTER (AND BEYOND)
## Desire Related Tasks

Now is the perfect time to schedule out the smaller tasks which get you closer to your larger goal. Write down all the necessary tasks you sense are needed to achieve your desire.

**If your desire / goal is still the same from the previous lunar cycle** then reflect on whether additional tasks may need to be assigned and write them here.

EXAMPLE:
Create a vision board to reflect my desire

MY DESIRE / GOAL:

Realistic Due date:

## TO DO NEXT...
Number all the tasks in order so you end up with a sequential timeline

MOONIFESTING

Date:

# FIRST QUARTER (AND BEYOND)

*Action Plan*

Now select the **first 3 tasks** and write down, in sequential order, the detailed steps (e.g. what you need, how many, who to contact etc.) and resources needed to achieve each task. Next, add a realistic timeframe of when you expect to have each step completed taking into account other life responsibilities. **Then actively DO THEM!** Once a step has been achieved, tick it off and celebrate! Any changes that need to be made to the steps can be completed in the Changes column which you can do anytime throughout the Lunar cycle.

## INFO

**TASK**
What is the task you need to complete to fulfill your desire?

**STEPS**
What steps do you need to take to complete the task?

**RESOURCES**
What resources will you need including material items, personal skills, and other people's involvement?

**DUE**
When can this step/s be realistically completed?

**CHANGES**
As you monitor your progress throughout the lunar cycle, are there any changes that may need to be made to the plan?

**DONE**
Tick each step once you have completed it and remember to CELEBRATE!

# FIRST QUARTER (AND BEYOND)
*Action Plan*

Date:

| TASK | STEPS | RESOURCES | DUE | CHANGES | DONE |
|------|-------|-----------|-----|---------|------|
|      |       |           |     |         |      |

Date:

# FIRST QUARTER (AND BEYOND)
*Action Plan*

| TASK | STEPS | RESOURCES | DUE | CHANGES | DONE |
|------|-------|-----------|-----|---------|------|
|      |       |           |     |         |      |

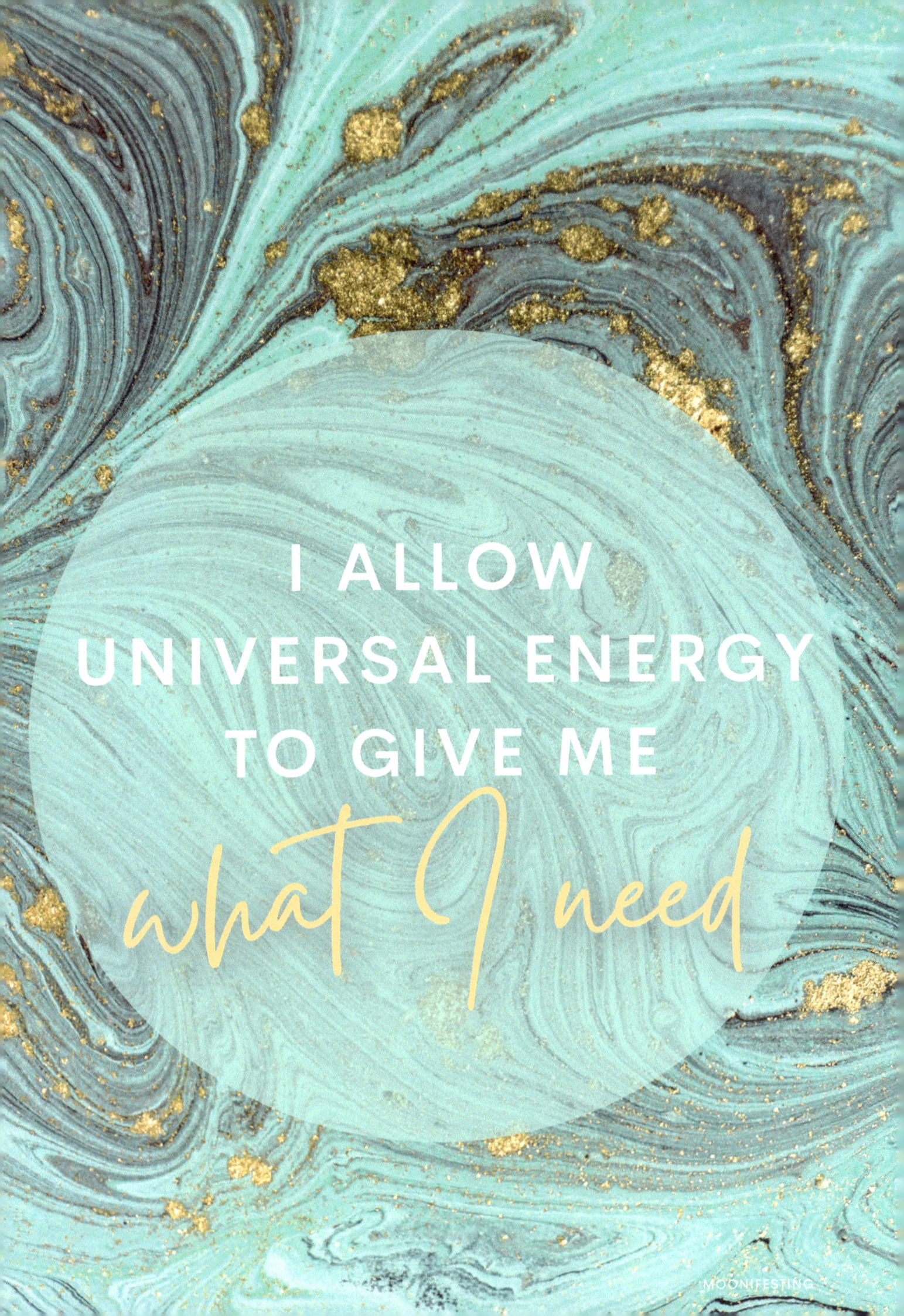

Date:

# WAXING GIBBOUS

REFINEMENT | REFOCUS | CHANGES | PATIENCE

Use this space to journal how you're feeling about the progress of your plan and the journey you have travelled so far including any milestones (big or small) that you have achieved.

My dreams are much more important than any fears I may have

Date:

# WAXING GIBBOUS
*This or something better...*

As you reflect on your progress so far whilst checking in with your inner guidance, are there any changes that need to be made to your action plan?

**Note:** *If the changes still relate to your current plan*, be sure to update the Changes column of your Action Plan. Trust that your plan and support from the Universe will take you to the finish line.

*If the changes no longer relate to your current plan (which is completely okay!)* then write or draw your new plan below and complete the Refined Action Plan on the following page.

Date:

# WAXING GIBBOUS (AND BEYOND)
*Refined Action Plan*

Write down **3 tasks** you could easily complete for the duration of this current lunar cycle and the associated steps needed to achieve each task. Remember to tick off each one once they're done and celebrate your progress!

| TASK | STEPS | RESOURCES | DUE | DONE |
|------|-------|-----------|-----|------|
|      |       |           |     |      |
|      |       |           |     |      |
|      |       |           |     |      |

Date:

# WAXING GIBBOUS (AND BEYOND)
*Refined Action Plan*

Write down **3 tasks** you could easily complete for the duration of this current lunar cycle and the associated steps needed to achieve each task. Remember to tick off each one once they're done and celebrate your progress!

| TASK | STEPS | RESOURCES | DUE | DONE |
|------|-------|-----------|-----|------|
|      |       |           |     |      |
|      |       |           |     |      |
|      |       |           |     |      |

Date:

# FULL MOON

RELEASE SETBACKS | CELEBRATE | SELF-LOVE

It's time to become aware of what needs to be seen and understood (Shadow Work) in order to release any setbacks. It's also a time to celebrate your beautiful nature and the magical life you're leading. As a gentle reminder (and if you haven't already) you may like to practice a specific Full Moon ritual (see The Moon Ritual section, particularly the Quick Moon Ritual Guide Step-by-Step section in this book which gives you all the information on how to do one) as a way of maintaining focus and connecting with the Full Moon's energy. Are you ready to go? Let's begin!

On this glorious journey of self love, have you forgiven yourself? If not, what do you need to forgive yourself for?

Finish this sentence (don't over think it, just answer it!): *Instead of worrying, I trust that no matter what happens I...*

*Keep reminding yourself of your own inner power*

Date:

# FULL MOON
## Oracle Card Spread

Record your Full Moon oracle spread here (if you feel called to do one) and consider how the messages that you receive can be applied to where you are in life right now and where you're going.

Date:

# FULL MOON
## Journaling Opportunity

"Place your hands into soil to feel grounded. Wade in water to feel emotionally healed. Fill your lungs with fresh air to feel mentally clear. Raise your face to the heat of the sun to connect with that fire and feel your own immense power" - *Victoria Erickson*

## Self Love Reminder

Find your self-love language: Your self-love language is how you show love to yourself, how you prefer to receive it, and what doesn't make you feel loved. Your own self-love language might be through touch such as massage, words or affirmations such as complimenting or cheering yourself on, acts of service which means setting things up or preparing something that you'll use later such as cleaning your bedroom so you can feel more relaxed, receiving gifts such as purchasing an online course or scheduling a haircut, and/or quality time which relates to spending productive time with yourself e.g. following a guided meditation or reading a new book. Whatever your self-love language is, ensure you make a point of expressing it every day.

Date:

# FULL MOON
## Shadow Work

Write a list or journal about all the things you're ready to let go of and why. You can also include those things that don't seem to relate to your overall plan. It's also a good idea to revisit the First Quarter section where you wrote about your fears and obstacles and consider if they're still relevant. The point is to just let it all out - don't hold back!

REMOVE THIS PAGE AND RIP IT UP OR BURN IT

Date:

# FULL MOON
## Shadow Work

REMOVE THIS PAGE AND RIP IT UP OR BURN IT

*I lovingly accept and release these shadows*

Hand on heart, do you acknowledge your part in this; that it is your choice to either let go of these shadows or hold onto them? If you ticked 'Yes', then sign and date below as a way of declaring your intention to accept, let these shadows go, and move on with confidence.

**Yes** ☐    **No** ☐

_____    _____
Your Signature                          Date

When you feel ready, burn or rip up this page as a symbol of release and liberation. Know that you are free of this energy that no longer serves your highest good.

Date:

# FULL MOON
## Journaling Opportunity

Now that you have released your shadows, you may like to sit in quiet contemplation and write or draw any thoughts, ideas, or impressions here.

I know and understand that my issues are how I am, not who I am

Date:

# WANING GIBBOUS

GRATITUDE | GIVE BACK | LOVE FULLY

Time can sometimes feel as though it's ticking by slowly or passing by quickly especially when we're immersed in doing something we love! Write down the people, things or experiences that you love and appreciate that you didn't have a year ago.

Date:

# WANING GIBBOUS

## Journaling Opportunity

Use this space to journal what has been revealed to you so far during this lunar cycle. With those revelations, you may like to consider what you'll do about them now, what you have learned so far, and how you can apply that to your intentions. It's also a good time to reflect on whether your goals are for the good of others as well as for yourself. And if things aren't turning out as planned, try to use your intuition to sense if you need to accept a different outcome.

Date:

# WANING GIBBOUS
*Journaling Opportunity*

This is the perfect time to share your positive vibes with others. Refer to the Give Back page of this journal and do one or more of the suggested activities. Spread those high-vibes dear soul!

Date:

# THIRD QUARTER

RELEASE | LET GO | FORGIVENESS

Throughout the lunar cycle you may have been hurt, disappointed, broken or angered in different ways, so now is the time to let go of any pent up emotions and negative thoughts that cause suffering.

Reflect on this lunar cycle. Is there any negative energy you need to and want to let go of? What do you need (if anything) to bring balance to yourself? Journal about it here.

*Journal Prompt*

How do you know when you have fully forgiven yourself or others? Is there anyone or any situation that you thought you'd forgiven but you know deep down there's still some residual energy to take care of?

MOONIFESTING

Date:

# THIRD QUARTER
## Journaling Opportunity

### Declutter Reminder
It's time to remove any distractions and excessive stress from your life. Refer to the Declutter portion of this book for ideas and inspiration on how to make space for the important things.

Date:

# THIRD QUARTER
## *Prayer to the Universe*

Sit somewhere comfortably where you won't be distracted. Take a few deep breaths to centre yourself. When you're ready read the following prayer to yourself slowly with the intention that this prayer is being directed to your soul and the Universe. You might like to do this a number of times as you allow the words to sink into your psyche. Try to *feel* into what the words represent for you. Lastly, say the prayer aloud as many times as you wish before finishing it off with another deep and cleansing breath.

**Note:** If you do not resonate with this prayer, then you may like to write your own for this particular Third Quarter Moon phase.

*The most amazing thing in my life right now is my present moment. I may have overlooked my present moment – unconsciously placing my awareness behind my past or toward my future. But here I am. There is never any other time than the time I have right now.*

*So as I breathe deeply with this awareness – this gift of presence, I automatically experience now. I acknowledge the way my life manifests around me. I appreciate the fullness of what is. I witness all that appears in the now - both what is outside of me and what is within me. I recognise and feel my aliveness. I am present within and present without. I ask that this moment be no different than anything it already is.*

*I take this deep breath in and recognise that I have come to myself – in the now, right now, in this moment.*

*And so it always is.*

Date:

# WANING CRESCENT

SURRENDER | REFLECTION | REST & RESTORE

As you bring closure to this lunar cycle, now is the perfect time to honour and love your strengths, realisations and accomplishments.

Reflect on how far you have come. Journal all the ways you have grown and what you have learned over the past lunar cycle.

Perform a bedtime ritual. Schedule a time when you'd like to go to bed then think of some things you'd like to do before you close your eyes. Perhaps you'd like to journal about your day, read a page from a good book, do some pre-sleep yoga moves or stretches, or simply listen to some peaceful music. Choose to do one or two things that help you wind down and relax.

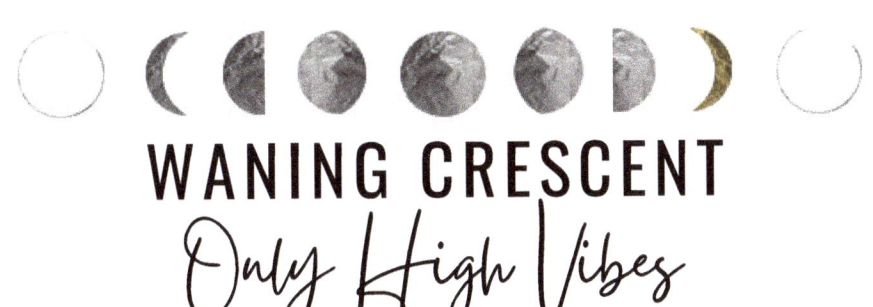

Date:

# WANING CRESCENT
*Only High Vibes*

If you sense your mind, body, spirit is in need of a positive energy boost, write down what you could do to bring about those high vibes and then actively do them!

_____     _____     _____
*Mind*                                    *Body*                                    *Spirit*

In addition to that, take some time to let your mind, body, spirit rest as you get creative by colouring in this mandala.

MOONIFESTING

Date:

# NOTES
*My Divine Space*

Date:

# NOTES
*My Divine Space*

Date:

# NOTES
*My Divine Space*

Date:

# NOTES
*My Divine Space*

Date:

# NOTES
*My Divine Space*

Date:

# NOTES
*My Divine Space*

Date:

# NOTES
*My Divine Space*

Date:

# NOTES
*My Divine Space*

Date:

# NOTES
*My Divine Space*

Date:

# NOTES
*My Divine Space*

# BEAUTIFUL SOUL
*Keep The Moonifesting Journey Going!*

Dear kindred spirit,

What a fabulous and wild ride you have had so far! I know there's been some ups and downs but it's how you have faced those times with courage, resilience and acceptance that matters. Hopefully with the help of this journal, you have come to love yourself more and aligned your way of living with the natural rhythms of the Moon whilst connecting to your own sacred wisdom.

Can you believe that this journal has been your spiritual counterpart throughout the past 6 lunar cycles?! It's helped you clear out some of the excess spiritual baggage and realigned your energy so you become a vibrational match to a life that's pretty darn good! But here's the thing - I truly don't want you to stop there! You've already got the ball rolling and have built the momentum around discovering who you are whilst attracting all that you desire and deserve - so keep going. The last thing you want to do is go back to a time when it was difficult to find happiness and peace. So make sure you grab another copy of Moonifesting to keep that beautiful momentum going!

I want to remind you that not only has this been a journey of manifesting what you ultimately wanted in life (so far) but it's also been a way of discovering just how powerful you are - that it's okay to play your own tune and step out of your comfort zone. This world needs your gifts so let them run free! We're at a pivotal time right now where your presence on Earth is wanted and needed so keep shining your light dear soul!

I am deeply thankful that you have chosen to walk this path and I hope you continue to grow and flourish into the ultimate version of yourself.

Lots of high-vibe love!